Wittgenstein's
Early Philosophy

Wittgenstein's Early Philosophy

Three Sides of the Mirror

Donald Peterson

University of Toronto Press
Toronto   Buffalo

First published in North America by
University of Toronto Press 1990
Toronto and Buffalo

Printed and bound in Great Britain

ISBN 0–8020–2770–9

Canadian Cataloguing in Publication data

Peterson, Donald M.
Wittgenstein's early philosophy

Includes bibliographical references.
ISBN 0–8020–2770-9

1. Wittgenstein, Ludwig, 1889–1951.   Tractatus
logico-philosophicus.   2. Languages – Philosophy.
3. Logic, Symbolic and mathematical.   I. Title.

B3376.W563T7347 1990   193   C90–093706–8

To Elizabeth

Contents

Acknowledgements

I am very grateful to the following for their comments on various parts and aspects of the developing manuscript: Elizabeth Anscombe, Roy Bhaskar, Oliver Black, Elizabeth Butler, Julian Coward, Antoni Diller, Alberto Emiliani, Barrie Falk, Chris Hookway, Hanna Lauterbach, Brian McGuinness, André Maury, Wolfgang Röhrl, Franziska Schössler, Arto Siitonen, Richard Verdi, and the members of the Cognitive Science Group at the University of Birmingham.

I am especially grateful to Erik Ameriller, John Watling, and Michael Wrigley for their extensive comments.

Abbreviations

Works by Wittgenstein

The translation given below of Wittgenstein's remarks in the *Tractatus* and in the *Notebooks* differ in places from those given by Pears and McGuinness, by Ogden, and by Anscombe, especially for the reasons given in the Appendix; but where there is no reason to differ, I have followed these translators. The page numbers given in references to the 'Notes on Logic' and the 'Notes Dictated to G. E. Moore in Norway' are those of the appendices in the *Notebooks 1914–1916* where these appear.

- N *Notebooks 1914–1916*.
- NL 'Notes on Logic' 1913, in *Notebooks 1914–1916*, as Appendix I.
- PT *Prototractatus*.
- T *Tractatus Logico-Philosophicus*.
- LE 'Lecture on Ethics'.
- PI *Philosophical Investigations*.
- CV *Culture and Value*.

Notes

- AN [Ambrose's Notes] *Wittgenstein's Lectures 1932–1935*, Alice Ambrose, ed.
- LN [Lee's Notes] *Wittgenstein's Lectures 1930–1932*, Desmond Lee, ed.

- MN1 [Moore's Notes 1] 'Notes Dictated to G. E. Moore in Norway', April 1914 in *Notebooks 1914–1916* as Appendix II.
- MN2 [Moore's Notes 2] 'Wittgenstein's Lectures in 1930–33', in G. E. Moore, *Philosophical Papers.*
- WN [Waismann's Notes] *Ludwig Wittgenstein and the Vienna Circle*, Brian McGuinness, ed.

Letters

- LO [Letters to Ogden] *Letters to C. K. Ogden.*
- LR [Letters to Russell *et al. Letters to Russell, Keynes, and Moore.*

Part I

INTRODUCTION

Chapter 1

The Conceptual Scheme of the Tractatus

Preliminaries

The *Tractatus Logico-Philosophicus* was first published in the original German in 1921, when its author, the Viennese Ludwig Wittgenstein, was 32. The book addresses the theory of linguistic representation: the relation between language and the world, those features internal to our representational systems, and those things beyond the reach of language—all of which are of central importance to philosophy, psychology, and nowadays to cognitive science. The *Tractatus* has a very marked character: it consists of an interconnected network of very terse, numbered remarks—some of which are given supporting argument, and some of which are dogmatically stated—covering a great variety of topics, and possessing a curious magic and fascination. In this compact form we find an atomistic ontology, a reductive analysis of representational language, discussions of the philosophy of logic, scientific theory, probability, modality and the nature of philosophy, together with myriad smaller points, and, finally, remarks on religion and the mystical.

However, what is most striking about the work is its obscurity: it is very hard indeed to see what the author is getting at, what he is up to, or where he is going. And the main reason for this obscurity is that the book's conceptual scheme—which provides the matrix within which all the particular points of argumentation are made—is not made explicit. It is this scheme which gives context, purpose, and

significance to the individual statements which compose the text,
and without it we are left with a heterogeneous and murky collection
of remarks.

The main purpose of the present exposition, then, is to explain
the contents of the *Tractatus* from its own perspective, and through
its own conceptual scheme.

Three Sides of the Mirror

At one point Wittgenstein called language the 'great mirror' (T 5.511,
cf N, p39). The subject of the *Tractatus* is the philosophy of language, or the general theory of representation, and what distinguishes the work is its concern with *all three sides of the mirror
of language*. It addresses the reflection or representation of the factual world in language. It addresses features which belong to the
inside of our representational mirror, and the illusion that these lie
outside it and are reflected in it. And it addresses the mystical realm
which lies behind the mirror of language, and cannot be reflected in
it.

The *Tractatus* is accordingly informed by a conceptual scheme
consisting of two threefold divisions. The first divides what is in
some sense real, and comprises (*1*) the world of facts, (*2*) the internal, 'syntactic' features of language, and (*3*) the ineffable 'mystical'
domain. The second, related, division concerns types of discourse,
and is composed of (*4*) representational, fact-stating discourse, (*5*)
discourse concerning the syntactic features of language, and (*6*) nonsense. Thus:

representational language	non-representational language	nonsense
the world of facts	the syntactic	the mystical

The *Tractatus* concerns both representation *and* non-representation: the theory of how language represents factual reality, and
of those things internal and external to language which cannot be
represented.

The general idea is this: we have a representational system and the target domain of reality which it can be used to describe—the world of facts. The representational system has its own inner 'syntactic' relations and necessities which are internal to it, and are not part of the target domain. If we use the representational system to talk about these, then, whether it is evident or not, we depart from the representation of facts, and use the language in a reflexive, non-representational manner. Lastly, there is the 'mystical' domain of what is real but which cannot be described at all in the representational system: attempts to do so are vacuous or 'nonsensical', as are statements which are intrinsically malformed.

The Primacy of the Scheme

This sixfold scheme is of primary importance to the *Tractatus*. It provides the grid through which the various topics are examined, and the context within which individual arguments are adduced; it determines the sorts of question which are addressed, and the types of thesis which are advanced and attacked. It gives point to the individual arguments, and continuity to an otherwise heterogeneous work.

When we turn to the contents of the *Tractatus* we find a complex web of argument: we are led straight into microscopic examination of individual and often technical points, whose significance and interrelation is frequently obscure. However, this complex, varying, and explicit web is woven over a simpler, constant, and implicit grid. And it is with reference to this grid that the purpose and relevance of Wittgenstein's various arguments and theses are to be found, as is the unity of the work.

As the *Tractatus* develops, emphasis is given to succeeding sides of the mirror, and accordingly to succeeding parts of the scheme. The first passages concern the nature of the factual world, and its description in representational language—the account being given in the atomistic ontology, the picture theory of meaning, and the theory of truth-functions. The middle passages largely concern the syntactic, and argue that various things belong there which might be thought to belong to the factual world, the most detailed examination being given to logic. And the final passages give brief attention to the mystical.

There is naturally room for variety within this framework: for example in representational language there are held to be features which are themselves ineffable, the inhabitants of the syntactic division are not wholly similar to one another, and nonsense can be produced by means other than attempting to describe the mystical. And as the text unfolds, various subsidiary issues are considered. But this is just to say that within the larger contours of the book, smaller contours are to be found.

The *Tractatus* gives an impression of unity: it initially seems to be a piece of charismatic but mysterious clockwork, though one senses that there is a spirit in the clockwork giving purpose to the parts and integrity to the whole. It is natural, then, to look for the source of this unity in some particular thesis or doctrine in the book: a cog which drives the rest of the machine, or an axel propelled by the whole. However the *Tractatus* does not in this sense have a centre: it does not have a main argument, a primary premise, or a principal conclusion. The book does not consist of the extended consequences and elaborations of some central driving doctrine, nor are its arguments organised so as all to determine some single result. What is essential to the book is not one of its particular theses, but the conceptual framework within which it is written—its unity derives not from a pivot but a matrix. And perhaps the best way of misunderstanding the work is to pick out one of its theses or arguments, to treat this as primary, and then to *reconstruct* the book accordingly.

The ontology and the picture theory of meaning are the best understood and the least believed doctrines of the *Tractatus*, and it has sometimes been thought that they constitute the book's centre. The ontology and the picture theory are bound up with one another, but, as will emerge below, the other doctrines of the *Tractatus* are actually largely independent of them. Wittgenstein's views on logic, scientific theory, the nature of philosophy, the mystical etc., do not depend on assumptions about the picture theory's analysis into *Elementarsätze* and the ontology's analysis into *Sachverhalte*. The relationship in question is one of compatibility rather than dependence, and if we reject the Tractarian account of representational language as Wittgenstein himself later did, this by no means entails a rejection of the other principal Tractarian doctrines.

There are nevertheless premises of considerable local importance, the most notable perhaps being those concerning the philosophy of logic, for example 4.0312 (the 'fundamental thought'), 5.551 (the 'fundamental principle'), and 6.113 (the 'whole philosophy of logic'), and due emphasis must be given to these (see chapter 6).

The *Tractatus* is not a book of '-isms', nor is it essentially opposed to a set of '-isms' to be found championed in the philosophical literature. Naturally many theses are asserted and denied in the course of the book, but insofar as the work as a whole is opposed to something, it is opposed to the perspective of Naïve Representationalism: the recognition in the theory of representation only of representational language and the factual world. Naïve Representationalism allows the mirror only one side, while the *Tractatus* allows it three. Thus the *Tractatus* differs from Naïve Representationalism not only in recognising that language has limits—that there are things which it cannot represent—but also in distinguishing the syntactic from the mystical, and accordingly in distinguishing the non-representational from the nonsensical uses of language.

The present interpretation is not essentially designed to trace the influences on Wittgenstein's thought of other philosophers and of the cultural *milieu* in which he grew up (though consideration is given to the influence of Hertz's mechanics on the Tractarian ontology and picture theory, and to Wittgenstein's reaction to Bertrand Russell's views on logic). Such factors are certainly important, and are well investigated elsewhere (see for example, Janik and Toulmin, 1973). However, although it is true, for example, that Wittgenstein's views on logic were to some extent a reaction against the axiomatic logic of Frege and Russell, and against a philosophy of logic which may naturally accompany this, and which Frege and Russell at times advocated, this reaction took place in *Wittgenstein's* terms, and from his own perspective. Russell's *Principles of Mathematics*, and Whitehead and Russell's *Principia Mathematica* certainly provided Wittgenstein with stimulus, as is clear in the *Tractatus*, but they did not provide him with the perspective from which he addressed the questions which they stimulated. As Wittgenstein said much later, 'Sow a seed in my soil and it will grow differently than in any other soil' (CV, p36); and although various of the views which Wittgenstein accepts or rejects in the *Tractatus* can be traced to Hertz, Frege, Russell, Schopenhauer and others, the soil, and the grid, within which these seeds grew were Wittgenstein's own.

Wittgenstein's Terminology

It is characteristic of Wittgenstein's style that, despite their importance, his scheme and his opposition to Naïve Representationalism are not clearly and explicitly impressed on the reader. We do however find him saying of the *Tractatus*:

> The main point is the theory of what can be expressed (gesagt) by propositions—that is by language—(and, which comes to the same thing, what can be *thought*) and what can not be expressed by propositions, but only shown (gezeigt) ; which, I believe, is the cardinal problem of philosophy. [LR, p71; Monte Cassino 19.8.1919]

and

> Its whole meaning could be summed up somewhat as follows: What can be said can be said clearly; and whereof one cannot speak thereof must one remain silent.
>
> The book will, therefore, draw a boundary to ... the expression of thoughts ... and what lies on the other side of the limit will simply be nonsense. [T, Preface]

Both of these statements express Wittgenstein's primary dual concern with representation and non-representation—both give first place to the idea that there are some cases where language can be used to describe something, and some where it cannot.

But neither statement is satisfactory, since neither distinguishes the syntactic from the mystical, nor the non-representational from the nonsensical. The *Tractatus* does not in fact draw a simple distinction between the describable and the indescribable, and a parallel simple distinction between descriptive and vacuous discourse. Rather, what does not belong to the factual world is further subdivided: there is the syntactic, comprising features and relations *internal* to language—and hence not external objects of depiction; and there is the mystical, comprising things *external* to language which by their nature cannot be described. And language which is not of the fact-stating sort is accordingly also further subdivided: there is talk about the syntactic—which in Wittgenstein's terminology is 'senseless'—and there is attempted talk about the mystical— which in Wittgenstein's terminology is 'nonsense'. It is for example most certainly not a doctrine of the *Tractatus* that logic—which is syntactic—is of the same sort as the aesthetic—which is mystical—and equally it is not suggested that the non-descriptive nature of talk about logic is the same thing as the non-descriptive nature of talk about the aesthetic.

It is, then, a sixfold rather than a fourfold scheme which informs the *Tractatus*, and it is unfortunate that Wittgenstein's remarks on the general perspective of his book are not only rare, but suggest a fourfold scheme, thus conveying the impression that the book is less sophisticated and less interesting than it actually is.

The sixfold scheme of the book is accurately mapped out by Wittgenstein's technical terminology. However, despite this blessing, it must be said that the terminology is peculiar and diverse: the expressions used do not have their usual meanings, either in the original German or in English translation, and in some cases several synonyms are used to express the same idea.

- Facts are, thankfully, referred to as 'facts' (*Tatsachen*), and the totality of these is the 'world' (*die Welt*). In the ontology facts are analysed into constituent 'elementary facts' (*Sachverhalte*). Facts can be 'said'.

- What has above been called the 'syntactic' is not given a collective name, although it is made clear that it comprises 'internal' features of, and relations within, sentences in representational language. (The expression 'syntax', for the symbols of a language together with the rules of their employment, appears more prominently after the period of the *Tractatus*—see WN.) The syntactic can be 'shown' but not 'said'.

- The domain of the ineffable is called the 'mystical'.

- Representational sentences are referred to simply as 'sentences' (*Sätze*), which 'say something', and have 'sense'. They comprise 'natural science', and express 'hypotheses', 'explanations', and 'doctrines': they describe the factual world. In the picture theory of meaning, sentences are analysed into 'elementary sentences' (*Elementarsätze*).

- Statements about syntactic matters such as logic are not 'sentences', they 'say nothing', and are 'senseless' (*sinnlos*) ; they do not constitute a 'science', and do not express 'doctrines' etc.—they concern not the factual world but the syntactic.

• Statements of the third type are 'nonsensical' (*unsinnig*) : statements which are made in the attempt to describe the mystical, or which treat something syntactic, such as identity, as if it belonged to the world of facts, or which are simply confused. The name 'pseudo-sentences' is given to statements which purport to be fact-stating, but which actually concern the syntactic or the mystical.

This terminology is used consistently, and does provide a handle on the Tractarian scheme. However, its peculiarity and its diversity do tend to disguise Wittgenstein's meaning and the continuity of his thought. If 'representational' or 'fact-stating' is appended as a prefix to 'sentence', 'science', 'doctrine' etc., and if 'sense' and 'say something' become 'factual sense', and 'say something factual', then the unity behind the diversity of Wittgenstein's terminology is brought out. For the sake of uniformity, discourse of the first type will here be called 'representational' or 'fact-stating', that of the second type will be called 'non-representational', and that of the third type will, with Wittgenstein, be called 'nonsensical'.

Overview

In interpreting the *Tractatus* it is advantageous to take an initial step back in order to identify the book's scheme and to avoid being bewitched by its terminology, both of which initially need to be gently decoupled from the actual contents of the book. The scheme is not stated *in* the book, but rather informs it—loosely speaking, it is not 'said' but 'shown'. Interestingly, the scheme is abstract enough that it is not tied to the precise contents of the *Tractatus*: within the same scheme, somewhat different topics could have been addressed, and different analyses advanced. If, for example, we reject the Tractarian ontology and the picture theory of meaning, this does not entail our rejecting the conceptual scheme, or the treatments of the syntactic and the mystical.

Part II below presents the Tractarian analyses of the factual world and representational language. Facts are composed of elementary facts, which in turn are composed of elementary objects.

Sentences are truth-functions of elementary sentences, which in turn are structures of elementary names. And language gets its grip on the world through the fundamental relation of depiction holding between elementary sentence and elementary fact.

Part III concerns the syntactic division and non-representational discourse. The syntactic is composed of 'internal' properties of and relations between representational sentences. To this category are assigned logic (which is discussed at the greatest length), identity, probability, modality, the subject matters of mathematics, scientific theory, and, rather more loosely, the causes of philosophical error. It is argued in the *Tractatus*, more fully in some cases than in others, that these concern features of language itself, rather than of anything outside language. Logical relations, for example, hold between sentences and not between facts, and a logical relation between two sentences holds because of the syntactic structures of those sentences, and not because of anything in the world.

Part IV concerns the mystical, and discourse of the nonsensical type. The mystical comprises what is ineffable—its occupants, although somehow real, cannot be described in language, and the attempt to talk about them results in 'nonsense'. According to the *Tractatus* these things must be 'passed over in silence', and among them are the 'ethical' (the realm of value), the aesthetic, and the religious.

It is argued again and again in the *Tractatus* that something belongs not to one category but to another. Some things, which look like facts of a universal or necessary character, turn out to be not factual but syntactic. And others, which look like facts of a sublime or elevated type, turn out to be not factual but mystical. In both cases what seem to be special facts, producing special reflections in the mirror, and studied by special sciences, turn out to be no facts at all.

The general result of the *Tractatus*, then, is to oppose Naïve Representationalism, and to establish the position in the theory of representation that the 'great mirror' of language has not one side but three.

Part II

REFLECTIONS IN THE MIRROR

Chapter 2

Configurations of Objects and Configurations of Names

Introduction

In its account of representational language and the world, the *Tractatus* has to explain *how sentences represent facts*. It has to explain *linguistic meaning* and description—what gives rise to the semantic relation of representation which allows language to talk *about* the world. This is achieved by giving parallel *atomistic analyses* of the world and representational language, and by maintaining that the essence of linguistic meaning is to be found in a relation of 'depiction' to be found at the lowest level of analysis. Sentences and facts as we normally know them are held not to be the basic bearers of meaning and the basic entities represented. Rather, these are analysed into their alleged constituents, and it is these constituents which are held to account for the representation of the world by language. Linguistic meaning is explained by moving one analytic step away from the phenomena of facts and sentences.

The Analysis of Facts

The analysis of the world is given in the ontology, which appears in the opening passages of the *Tractatus*. The world is declared, by definition, to be the totality of facts (*Tatsachen*). These facts

15

break down into 'elementary facts' (*Sachverhalte*)[1], and these in turn consist in configurations of 'objects' (*Gegenstände*).

> The world is the totality of facts, not of things. [T 1.1]

> What is the case—a fact—is the existence of of elementary facts. [T 2]

> An elementary fact is a combination of objects (entities, things). [T 2.01]

The basic constituents of the factual world are elementary facts, and an elementary fact has two aspects: (*1*) the objects which compose it, and (*2*) the configuration in which these are arranged:

> The configuration of objects forms the elementary fact. [T 2.0272]

> The determinate way in which objects are connected in an elementary fact is the structure of the elementary fact. [T 2.032]

The world, then, consists ultimately of elementary facts:

> The totality of existing elementary facts is the world. [T 2.04]

And in explaining linguistic meaning, it has to be explained how language represents these configurations of elementary objects.

The Analysis of Representational Sentences

The breakdown of representational language proceeds in parallel to that of the world. Representational language is the totality of representational sentences ('sentences', or *Sätze* in the Tractarian terminology):

> The totality of sentences is language. [T 4.001]

---

[1]The issues surrounding the translation of the German terms *Tatsache*, *Sachverhalt*, *Satz*, and *Elementarsatz* are discussed in the Appendix.

And the sum of all true representational sentences is called 'natural science':

> The totality of true sentences is the whole of natural science (or the whole corpus of the natural sciences). [T 4.11]

Representational sentences break down into elementary sentences (*Elementarsätze*)[2], which are configurations of names (*Namen*):

> It is obvious that the analysis of sentences must bring us to elementary sentences which consist of names in immediate combination. [T 4.221]

Thus, the basic constituents of representational language are elementary sentences, and an elementary sentence has two aspects: (*1*) the names which compose it, and (*2*) the configuration in which these are arranged:

> An elementary sentence consists of names. It is a nexus, a concatenation of names. [T 4.22]

The fundamental case of representation is the depiction of an elementary fact by an elementary sentence:

> If an elementary sentence is true, the elementary fact exists: if an elementary sentence of false, the elementary fact does not exist. [T 4.25]

Representational language is ultimately composed of elementary sentences, and the world is completely described by the totality of true elementary sentences:

> If all true elementary sentences are given, the result is a complete description of the world ... [T 4.26]

Thus, given this dual analysis of the world and representational language, what is required in order to explain linguistic meaning is an explanation of how an elementary sentence represents an elementary fact.

---

[2]The nature of this (truth-functional) breakdown will be discussed in the following chapter

Linguistic Meaning

The explanation of the essential representational connection between elementary sentence and elementary fact is provided by what commentators have called the 'picture theory of meaning'. In his exposition, Wittgenstein is unusually repetitive, and somewhat oblique, since his discussion concentrates on a general account of 'pictures' (*Bilder*) rather than a specific account of elementary sentences, but his main lines of thought are clear.

The essential idea is that the basic representational relation of depiction has two aspects: (*1*) that the elements in the picture (the names in an elementary sentence) correspond to the elements in the situation depicted (the objects in an elementary fact), and (*2*) that the structure of the picture (the configuration of names in an elementary sentence) be the same as the structure of the situation depicted (the configuration of objects in the elementary fact). Thus:

> In a picture the elements of the picture are the representatives of objects. [T 2.131]

and

> That the elements of a picture are related to one another in a determinate way represents that things are related to one another in the same way.

> Let us call this connection of its elements the structure of the picture ... [T 2.15]

There is a relation of depiction between a picture and a situation when the elements of the two are paired off, and the structures of the two are the same. It is emphasised that the second—structural—aspect is necessary: that naming of objects is not enough:

> A sentence is not a mixture of words.—(Just as a theme in music is not a mixture of notes.) ... [T 3.141; cf N, p96]

And in a letter to C.K. Ogden he explains that he means that a sentence is ' ... no MIXTURE but a STRUCTURE' (LO, p24). That is, a mere set of names cannot depict a situation or elementary fact: the required configuration must be present also.

The elementary sentence is likened to a picture. In a picture—
a painting, a photograph etc.—there are elements in a (spatial)
arrangement, and these match entities in the corresponding scene
which are arranged in the same configuration. Analogously, an elementary sentence consists of names in a configuration, and if the
sentence is true there exists an elementary fact composed of objects
named by these names and arranged in a corresponding configuration. When names and objects correspond to one another, and
the required structural affinity obtains between elementary sentence
and elementary fact, then the elementary sentence stands for the
elementary fact.

The world is analysed into elementary facts, and representational
language is analysed into elementary sentences, and at this ultimate level of analysis linguistic meaning is created through the joint
agency of the *naming relationship* and *structural affinity*. This, together with the theory of truth-functions (see chapter 3), constitute
the essentials of the early Wittgenstein's account of representational
language and the world: his account of the inhabitants of the first
two divisions in his scheme. And it is against this background that he
later moves on to consideration of the syntactic, non-representational
language, the mystical, and nonsensical language. In pursuing these
further topics, the terminology and outlook developed in this initial
analysis certainly carry through, but, as will be argued below, his
further analyses do not intrinsically depend on the *atomistic* character of his account of representation: they can be formulated without
reference to elementary facts, elementary sentences, elementary objects, or elementary names.

Hertz's Mechanics

Wittgenstein is known to have taken considerable interest in Heinrich
Hertz's *Principles of Mechanics*, and Hertz is mentioned by name in
two places in the *Tractatus*. As James Griffin says:

> The picture theory comes almost in its entirety from Hertz. Witt-
> genstein was the first perhaps, to apply a picture theory of mean-
> ing to the whole of language, but not the first to apply it to a part.
> [*Wittgenstein's Logical Atomism*, p99]

Wittgenstein's may have first encountered Hertz's ideas through the discussion of Hertz's mechanics which appears in chapter *LIX* of Russell's *Principles of Mathematics*, or perhaps while he was a student in Berlin (see McGuinness, *Wittgenstein: A Life*). In any case, the main elements of Wittgenstein's picture theory are all to be found in Hertz's mechanics—this concerns 'configurations' or 'systems' of 'material points', the 'pictures' or 'models' (*Bilder*) we make of these configurations, and the structural isomorphism between picture and configuration. Thus:

> Every material particle is invariable and indestructible. [*Principles of Mechanics*, §3]

> A material point therefore consists of any number of material particles connected with each other. [*op cit*, §4]

> A number of material points considered simultaneously is called a system of material points, or briefly a system. [*op cit*, §5]

> The aggregate of the relative positions of the points of a system is called the configuration of the system. [*op cit*, §14]

> The relation of the dynamical model to the system of which it is regarded as a model, is precisely the same as the relation of the images which our mind forms of things themselves ... The agreement between mind and nature may therefore be likened to the agreement between two systems which are models of one another, and we can even account for this agreement by assuming that the mind is capable of making actual dynamical models of things, and of working with them. [*op cit*, §428]

Hertz's theory involves four levels (those of particles, points, systems of points, and dynamical models of these systems), whereas Wittgenstein's theory involves only three levels (those of objects, elementary facts, and pictures). Nevertheless the similarity between the two theories is striking, and Hertz can be regarded as a primary influence on this aspect of Wittgenstein's early thought. And given the strength and detail of this influence, there may be less importance than has been thought in the occasion when Wittgenstein read in a newspaper of the representation in a Parisian court of a car accident by means of dolls, model cars etc. (see von Wright in Malcolm,

1984, pp7–8, and N p7). This may have been the occasion when Wittgenstein conceived the general picture theory of meaning, but the source of the idea seems to be in Hertz's writings, which he had already read.

Hertz's influence extends beyond Wittgenstein's picture theory. As J. Griffin points out (*op cit*, pp102–8) Wittgenstein's idea, expressed in the 6.3's in the *Tractatus*, that many general scientific statements are about our mode of representation of the world, and not about the world itself may be traced to Hertz (cf *op cit*, §421). And as P.M.S. Hacker (*Insight and Illusion*, p4) says, the concern with pseudo-problems can also found in Hertz (*op cit*, Introduction, pp7f). The present point, though, is that the main elements in the picture theory and its associated ontology are to be found in Hertz's writings.

Some Details of the Ontology

The ontological atomism which Wittgenstein puts forward in the *Tractatus* bears some similarity to that advanced by Leucippicus and Democritus in the 5th century BC: the substance of the world consists of simple and changeless objects (atoms), facts are arrangements of these fundamental constituents, and all change consists in rearrangement of the world's objects.

In the *Tractatus* objects are held to be simple, indivisible, and unchanging: they cannot be broken down, they do not alter in themselves, and presumably their number is constant. In this sense, they constitute what Wittgenstein called the 'substance' of the world (T 2.021). However the world as a whole does of course change, and this change consists in *rearrangement* of the objects. It is rather as if a set of children's building-bricks were used to construct a series of different buildings: the arrangement of the bricks would change over time, but the set of bricks themselves would remain constant.

> Objects are what is unalterable and subsistent; their configuration is what is changing and unstable. [T 2.0271; cf 2.0124, 2.014, 2.02, 2.021, 2.024]

Looking from the point of view of an object, this has the possibility of combining with others to form various configurations—various

elementary facts. And these constitute the set of configurations into
which the object might enter. Thus:

> Each thing is, as it were, in a space of possible elementary facts
> ... [T 2.013].

We encounter here Wittgenstein's use of the word 'space' to mean
a determinable.[3] The general notion of a determinable (see W.E.
Johnson, 1921) is the notion of a set of possibilities, exactly one of
which must obtain at any given time. Thus colours form a determinable in the sense that at any one time a given speck must have
exactly one colour. Temperatures constitute a determinable in that,
at any one time, a given point on a physical body must have exactly
one temperature. Physical space is a determinable in the sense that,
given a set of defining coordinates, a point on a physical body must
at any one time be in exactly one place: it cannot be in more than
one place at a time, and it cannot be nowhere (cf T 2.0131).

Just as a point on a physical body is surrounded by a space
of places it is not but could have been, so, figuratively, it is surrounded by spaces of colours, temperatures etc., which it does not
have but might have had. In each case the determinable, or 'space',
includes the actualised possibility, together with those which at the
moment do not obtain. In this sense a given Tractarian object is
'surrounded' by the 'space' of all possible worlds: the set of all possible arrangements of the totality of objects. And this set of options,
through which the world moves as it changes, is determined by the
unchanging set of objects of which these arrangements are composed
(cf T 2.0124).

This brings out an interesting aspect of the Tractarian ontology.
The notion of a determinable or 'space' brings with it the notion of
exclusion: whatever possibility obtains excludes all the others, and
so we might expect that an object's appearance in one arrangement
would exclude its simultaneous appearance in another. The question
is at what level this exclusion obtains. Objects combine in the first
place into elementary facts, and so we might expect these accordingly
to exclude one another. But Wittgenstein denies this, asserting that
the existence of one elementary fact has no bearing on the existence
or non-existence of others (T 2.061, 2.062) (see chapter 5). Thus he

---

[3]For an analysis of Wittgenstein's conception of 'logical space', see Peterson,
1986a.

implies that if an object appears in one elementary fact, this does not in itself exclude its simultaneous appearance in another quite different one. And if we move up to the level of facts (*Tatsachen*) we find the same thing: 'Each can be the case or not the case, while the others remain the same' (T 1.21). It is only at the level of the world as a whole that exclusion is allowed between one macro-arrangement of objects and another:

> ... the totality of facts determines what is the case, and also whatever is not the case. [T 1.12]

But by the time we reach this level, a statement of exclusion becomes vacuous, since it is a matter of definition that we are dealing with *all* the facts—the whole of reality, the total arrangement of objects—and hence that no other arrangement simultaneously exists.

Elementary facts, then, are independent: the existence of one cannot exclude the existence of another, and, it seems, the appearance of an object in one cannot exclude its simultaneous appearance in another. Thus the 'space' or determinable which surrounds an object is not a set of possible elementary facts, but rather a set of possible worlds.

A further point of interest is that Tractarian objects are held to be indescribable:

> Objects can only be *named*. Signs are their representatives. I can only speak *about* them: I cannot *put them into words*. [T 3.221; cf N, p51]

This can be seen as a consequence of Wittgenstein's other views: the picture theory reduces the number of grammatical categories involved in an elementary sentence to one—that of names. All component signs in an elementary sentence are names, and the function of all names is to 'go proxy' for objects. Thus if we restrict our subject matter to one object, we cannot do more than name it: if we do more than this we must use other words (names) and so we expand our subject matter. Antisthenes the Cynic (c. 445–365 BC) put forward a similar argument as an attack on the Socratic practice of searching for definitions. E. Kapp summarises the argument:

> With a single word you can only name a thing, but in order to say what is, or what was, you have to form a sentence. Now, a sentence

is by its very nature a combination of words. In a combination of
words you can obviously express your knowledge of a combination
of things, but it is equally obvious that it is nonsense to try to
say one thing in a combination of words ... A single thing can
only be named, no statement as to what it is or what it is not
can be made, because stating consists in using a combination of
words and a combination of words simply does not fit a single
noncombined object. [Kapp, 1942, p53]

The point for Antisthenes is that if an attempt is made to define
something which we take to be simple, then we must fail, since the
definiens will be complex and so will not 'fit' the simple *definiendum*.
Courage, piety, friendship, *areté* etc. are simple, and so can be
named but no more. And the point for Wittgenstein is analogous.

Some Details of the Picture Theory

The notion of an *internal relation* is important in Wittgenstein's
thought and is mentioned in several of his remarks. By an internal
relation he means one between two things which is given as soon
as the two things are given: one which holds independently of external assistance and in this sense 'takes care of itself' —a relation
which holds solely in virtue of the structures of those two things,
and therefore obtains automatically as soon as the two things exist. The concept arises in Wittgenstein's discussions of the relation
between elementary sentence and elementary fact, and also in his
treatment of the logical relations which hold between one sentence
and another (see chapter 6); and in both cases what is involved is a
relation between structures.

According to the picture theory of meaning, there is an internal,
structural relation between an elementary sentence in language and
the elementary fact which it depicts in the world. In the 4's Wittgenstein says:

A gramophone record, the musical idea, the written notes, and the
sound waves all stand to one another in the same internal relation
of depicting that holds between language and the world. [T 4.014]

A sentence communicates a situation to us, and so it must be
essentially connected with the situation. [T 4.03]

Compare:

> ...language stands in *internal* relations to the world. [N, pp42–3]

> The internal relation between the sentence and its reference, the method of symbolising—is the system of co-ordinates which projects the situation into the sentence. The sentence corresponds to the fundamental co-ordinates. [N, p20]

Given an elementary fact, the corresponding elementary sentence, and naming relations between names and objects established by 'arbitrary convention', the relation of depiction is automatic, and is given as soon as these things are given, and requires no additional factor external to sentence and fact. The pairing off of names and objects, and the structural affinity between sentence and fact, together ensure that one depicts the other:

> In this way the sentence represents the situation—as it were off its own bat. [N, p26]

> We must recognise *how* language takes care of itself ...I cannot need to worry about language. [N, p43]

It must be assumed of course that the names and objects have been paired off by naming conventions, and this circumstance is external to the written or spoken sentence and to the fact, but the formal component is not a matter of convention and is internal to sentence and fact, and so given the naming relations as a background, depiction is automatic—it takes place 'off its own bat', and 'takes care of itself'.

A further point is that the formal component of the picture—that which is common to elementary sentence and elementary fact—cannot itself be represented in language:

> Sentences can represent the whole of reality, but they cannot represent what they must have in common with reality in order to be able to represent it—logical form. [T 4.12]

Thus the forms of elementary facts and elementary objects (T 3.221), both of which belong to the world, cannot be described in

language: the representational picturing relation is based on factors
which themselves elude description.

Finally, Wittgenstein mentions in several places that the mathematical 'multiplicity' of the elementary sentence must be equal to
that of the elementary fact depicted, which is a rather grand way
of saying that these must contain the same number of components.
The point is that since the elementary sentence is a configuration
of names depicting a configuration of objects, it is required that the
names in the elementary sentence and the objects in the elementary fact be properly paired off. The picture should not have extra
elements (names) nor missing elements:

> In a sentence there must be exactly as many distinguishable parts
> as in the situation that it represents. The two must possess the
> same logical (mathematical) multiplicity. (Compare Hertz's *Me-
> chanics* on dynamical models.) [T 4.04]

Hertz had, as suggested, made a similar point:

> A material system is said to be a dynamical model of a second
> system when the connections of the first can be expressed by such
> co-ordinates as to satisfy the following conditions:- (*1*) That the
> number of co-ordinates of the first system is equal to the number
> of the second ... [*Principles of Mechanics*, §418]

This implies, presumably, that in an elementary sentence there
can be no co-referential names. In ordinary language, a sentence may
have more than one name-token of the same name-type, and further
co-reference is created through pronouns and definite descriptions.
But at the elementary level we can have none of this: in the interests
of structural isomorphism, there must be one name per object.

Problems

Projection

Despite its appearance of formal elegance, Wittgenstein's exposition
does not have the happy simplicity we might hope for. For example when we look for further explanation of the internal relation
between picture and fact, we are told that a picture 'reaches right

out' to reality (T 2.1511), that it is 'laid against reality like a measure' (T 2.1512), and there is mention of 'graduating lines', 'correlations' (T 2.1514), and 'feelers' (T 2.1515). These are uninstructive metaphors which do little to illuminate the issue.

The theory is further complicated when Wittgenstein says that the 'method of projection' from sentence to 'possible situation' is to 'think the sense of the sentence' (T 3.11; cf T 4.0141). The *Tractatus* is remarkably devoid of any mention of the rôle of the mind in establishing linguistic meaning, but here we find a psychological concept being introduced without explanation.[4]

Concerning the nature of the structure common to sentence and fact, Wittgenstein's guiding metaphor was evidently a spatial one:

> The essence of the sentential sign is very clearly seen if we imagine one composed of spatial objects (such as tables, chairs, and books) instead of signs. Then the spatial arrangement of these things will express the sense of the sentence. [T 3.1431; cf N, p15]

But, to state the obvious, although normal sentences may be *like* pictures, they are not literally pictures: a sentence written on a page, such as this one, is not a photograph, a drawing, a painting, etc. Sentences have grammatical and semantic characteristics which pictures do not have, and unlike pictures they belong to languages such as English, German, or French. And in a real picture the structural component is quite literally a spatial arrangement, but this can hardly be maintained with respect to a sentence written on a page, or spoken out loud.

Wittgenstein was essentially concerned with elementary sentences rather than with the sentences of ordinary language, but by moving down to the elementary level he does not avoid the problem of explaining the nature of the relevant structures. In particular, if the arrangement of elementary names were spatial, then the elementary sentences would have to exist in space, and then we would want to know *where* they were—for they seem to be nowhere. And accordingly, in this case the equivalent configuration of elementary objects in the elementary fact would also have to be spatial, and again we would want to know where these were to be found. It must be conceded that the German *Bild*, here translated as 'picture', can

---

[4]For an investigation of this issue see Hacker's *Insight and Illusion*, 1972 edition, chapter II, part 2.

equally be translated as 'model', in which case the implication of *spatial* structure is not so great. However we still need structure or form of *some* sort, and it seems that if we refuse to carry over more than is reasonable from the pictorial metaphor, we are left without explanation of the crucial structural component in this account of representation (see also epilogue I).

Analysis

In following this double analysis of language and the world, we have left the realm of facts and sentences as we normally know them.

Nobody has ever seen an elementary fact, and equally nobody has ever seen a Tractarian object: they are theoretical postulates of Wittgenstein's account, and are to be encountered neither in everyday experience nor in the findings of science. This is atomistic ontology at its most abstract. The Tractarian objects are not of course the clocks, billiard balls, teaspoons, and refrigerators we normally find around us, and neither are they the molecules, atoms, electrons etc. to which physics reduces these. Rather, they are the mysterious ultimate constituents of facts, not of things.

Similarly, nobody has ever read, heard, written, or spoken an elementary sentence—nor uttered nor heard a Tractarian elementary name. These are again theoretical postulates of Tractarian analysis, and are not to be found in language as we experience it. Tractarian atomism is, like the physicist's, an atomism of the invisible, but in contrast to the case of physics there is no evidence of the existence of the supposed end-products of this analysis.[5]

In the *Notebooks*, Wittgenstein discusses several difficulties. One major and predictable problem is the absence of examples: there are no cases of successful analysis, no examples of objects, names of objects, elementary facts, or elementary sentences. For example:

> My difficulty consists in this: In all the sentences that occur to me there occur names, which, however must disappear on further analysis. I know that such a further analysis is possible, but am unable to carry it out completely ... In brief it looks as if in this

---

[5]For an attempt to derive from the *Tractatus* a reductive argument to the conclusion that elementary objects *must* exist, see D. Pears, *The False Prison*, vol. 1, chapter 4.

way I knew a form without being acquainted with a single example of it. [N, p61; cf T 5.55, 5.555, 5.5562–71]

In lieu of actual examples of objects etc., it is suggested in the *Notebooks* that their existence can be inferred:

> But it also seems certain that we do not infer the existence of simple objects from the existence of particular simple objects, but rather know them—by description, as it were—as the end-product of analysis, by means of a process that leads to them. [N p50]

Thus, the ontology and the picture theory of meaning are advanced in the absence of actual examples of elementary objects, elementary names etc., and in the absence of any specification of the sort of analysis which might provide these.

Wittgenstein does remark that the process of analysis will be futile if objects are infinitely divisible, in which case we will never arrive at a simple, indivisible ontological atom.

> And nothing seems to speak against infinite divisibility.

> *And it keeps on* forcing itself upon us that there is some simple indivisible, an element of being, in brief a thing. [N, p62]

And even more worrying than the suggested impossibility of performing the required analysis is the observation that it seems superfluous.

> But this is surely clear: the sentences which are the only ones that humanity uses will have a sense just as they are and do not wait upon a future analysis in order to acquire sense. [N, p62]

This is a telling point: human beings understand one another's meanings already, and yet we cannot provide an analysis which converts the sentences we use into sentences to which the picture theory can be applied directly; thus if such an analysis says what sentences *really mean*, we are led to the improbable conclusion that we have an *implicit* or unconscious understanding of it.

Another problem for Tractarian analysis is that of explaining how a single word can play the rôle of a true declarative sentence, as it can in a code: the word is simple, and yet there is at least some measure of complexity in the fact depicted by it, and this seems to violate the requirement that the two be structurally similar.

...how is it possible for 'kilo' in a code to mean: 'I'm all right'?
Here surely *a simple sign* does assert something and is used to give
information to others. [N, p8]

It might be suggested that although 'kilo' is a structurally simple
sentence, the fully analysed sentence would be complex. But it is
hard to see how the simple sequence of four letters 'k', 'i', 'l', and 'o'
could lead to such an analysis. Surely the analysis of 'kilo' could only
take place on the basis of a knowledge of its meaning (for example, its
meaning in the code might be that troops are advancing to the north
of the town). But this is to use the meaning to explain the structure,
whereas it is the structure which should explain the meaning.

Creation or Discovery?

It is worth noting that for the Tractarian atomism to be credible,
analysis must be a process of discovery rather than a process of
creation. If language actually does—rather than could or should—
represent the world through elementary sentences which directly depict elementary facts, then it is required that these should exist in
order to perform their function.

If someone utters a sentence, we can *deduce* from it a second sentence which did not exist before. In Russell's Theory of Descriptions
(Russell, 1905), a sentence is analysed so as to derive a second sentence in the predicate calculus (the second sentence being more perspicuous and less misleading than the first). Russell's idea no doubt
influenced Wittgenstein, but an analogous account will not do in the
case of *Elementarsätze*, since in order to play their rôle of depicting
elementary facts, they must exist *now*—it is not enough that we
might be able to derive them by analysis. In Russell's method, we
create a new sentence, and so discover the meaning of the first one,
while in Wittgenstein's, if we had it, we would *discover* elementary
sentences which had existed all along.

Summary

The Tractarian ontology and picture theory of meaning have great
formal beauty, and manifest tenacious consistency in the development of the original Herzian ideas. However, examination of their

substance quickly leads to myriad problems—the Tractarian account of linguistic meaning is perhaps just too elegant to be realistic.

It is not my present purpose to examine or criticise the ontology and the picture theory at length[6], but to bring out the main lines of thought they embody. Prescinding from the details of the theories, and from their problems, their principal theses are (*1*) that the components of a (true) elementary sentence are *names* which stand for objects in the elementary fact depicted, (*2*) that an *internal relation of structural isomorphism* obtains between elementary sentence and elementary fact, and (*3*) that the form common to elementary sentence and elementary fact is not itself describable in language.

We might expect that, having characterised the world of facts and representational language, Wittgenstein would then use the details of this account to demarcate the inhabitants of the other sectors in his scheme. We might expect him to use his account of facts in explaining the non-factual nature of the denizens of the syntactic and mystical realms. And again we might expect him to use the details of his theory of representational language in arguing that certain types of utterance are non-representational or nonsensical. Surprisingly, he does not do this—the exception being that, as discussed in chapter 9, he thought that by demarcating the realm of the factual he had thereby demarcated the realm of the mystical.

Of course, the terminology of these early passages is to be found throughout the *Tractatus*. And when the Logical Independence Thesis is formulated, it is stated in terms of *elementary* facts. But the influence goes no further: as will be seen, the rest of the *Tractatus* has nothing to do with analysis down to isomorphic configurations of elementary names and elementary objects. And whenever an argument later in the *Tractatus* mentions elementary sentences or elementary facts, one finds that this is irrelevant, and that the force of the argument is directed to representational sentences or facts *in general*. In particular, there is nothing in the argumentative support given to the *Grundgedanke* or the Logical Independence Thesis which shackles these to the Tractarian ontology or picture theory: what is really proven is that facts in general are devoid of logical constants and are logically independent, not just that elementary facts enjoy these features. The doctrines expressed in the middle

---

[6]For further detailed treatment of this part of the *Tractatus*, see Black, *Companion*; Hacker, *Insight and Illusion*; and Pears, *The False Prison*, vol. 1.

and later passages of the *Tractatus* are atomistic only in the sense that they demonstrate that facts in general are logically *independent*—indeed logically vacuous—they do not rely on or support the parallel *reductions* perpetrated by the ontology and the picture theory of meaning.

The ontology and the picture theory, then, do not constitute the basis of the *Tractatus*—the Tractarian rainbow does not consist of variations of green and blue. The book simply does not have the axiomatic character which has sometimes been sought in it, and as already mentioned, we are free to reject the earlier passages and retain the later ones.

The issue of projection can be seen as the Achilles' heel of the Tractarian account of representation. What has to be explained, after all, is the projection of language onto the world: *meaning, aboutness, description, representation.* Our sentences are *about* the world—they describe it. The Tractarian explanation of this is that at the level of an elementary code, representation takes place through naming and through an internal relation of structural isomorphism. When names and objects correspond, and the structures are the same, the semantic spark jumps the gap, and meaning is born. The great virtue of such a theory is that it purports to provide a *semantic terminus*—a level at which representation obtains automatically. The relation of structural isomorphism is therefore at once a point of strength and vulnerability in Wittgenstein's account of representation: if this internal relation is made credible, then the theory explains a lot, but if not, then the theory falls.

Wittgenstein later abandoned this view, arguing, essentially, that language describes the world through language-games, rather than through the metaphysical matching of the picture theory. And this lends something to the already easy task of finding fault with and dismissing the picture theory. But the picture theory has great value, not because it is correct—which it is not—but because Wittgenstein articulated and developed the details and consequences of such theories of meaning. His work, and subsequent criticism, have made it plain what is the appeal and what are the faults of such a theory, and in particular, they have emphasised that a theory of this sort relies essentially on an internal, and presumably structural, relation between elementary sentence and elementary fact. And in examining, for example, the conceptual basis of cognitive science, we find that, in theories of 'mental representation' inspired by the computer model of the mind, the picture theory and its internal relation are not dead (see epilogue I).

We now turn to the theory of truth-functions, which plays two principal rôles in the *Tractatus*: it completes the analysis of representational language (see the following chapter), and it is used in establishing that logic is syntactic in nature (see chapter 6).

Chapter 3

Truth-Functions

Introduction

The *Tractatus* contains no logical technicality which is presented for its own sake: rather each is presented because of its significance for some philosophical point. In the case of the theory of truth-functions, the targets are two related issues in the philosophy of logic.

First, with regard to representational language, the theory of truth-functions is used to explain the seemingly anomalous rôle of the logical constants or connectives in fact-stating discourse. The constants are expressions such as 'and', 'or', 'not', 'if ... then ... ', 'all', 'some' etc., or their counterparts in logical notation: on the one hand these *do not name objects in the world*, but on the other hand they do appear in representational discourse. If I say 'The cat is on the mat *or* it is on the chair', I am talking about objects called 'cat', 'mat', and 'chair' in the world, but I am *not* talking about an object called 'or'. Their place in fact-stating language therefore cannot be explained by the picture theory of meaning alone, and in this context the theory of truth-functions augments the picture theory and so completes the Tractarian explanation of fact-stating discourse.

Second, the theory of truth-functions is used to give substance to the thesis that logic is syntactic: the logical properties and relations are analysed through the theory of truth-functions, demonstrating that these are properties of and relations between *sentences themselves*, rather then anything subsisting externally to the great mirror.

The thesis that the logical connectives are not names of objects is given and substantiated by the *Grundgedanke* (T 4.0312) and its supporting arguments. This motivates the theory of truth-functions, and also leads to the Logical Independence Thesis, which itself supports the thesis that logic is syntactic. And, as already mentioned, the thesis that logic is syntactic is given technical detail by the theory of truth-functions. The structure of argument here is therefore involved and non-linear, and cannot be flattened-out in exposition. The technical details of the theory of truth-functions, and its bearing on representational language will be described in the present chapter. The *Grundgedanke*, the thesis that logic is syntactic, and the application of the theory of truth-functions to this thesis will be examined in chapters 4, 5, and 6.

The Theory of Truth-Functions

The immediate purpose of the theory of truth-functions is to explain the rôle of the logical connectives: alternatively put, its purpose is to explain logically molecular sentences (those which contain logical constants), as distinct from logically atomic sentences (those which contain no logical constants).

The technical details of the theory of truth-functions are well known, though Wittgenstein's exposition is naturally coloured by the terminology and concerns of the *Tractatus*.

The logically atomic components of a sentence generate a set of *truth-possibilities*. For n component sentences there are 2^n truth-possibilities. Thus for 1 component sentence there are 2 truth-possibilities, for 2 there are 4, for 3 there are 8, for 4 there are 16 etc. The four truth-possibilities associated with the component sentences 'p' and 'q', can be tabulated as:

	p	q
1	T	T
2	T	F
3	F	T
4	F	F

The compound sentence will agree with some of these truth-possibilities, and it will disagree with others: some will make the sentence true, and some will make it false. The pattern of 'agreement and disagreement' with truth-possibilities is the set of *truth-conditions* of a sentence (T 4.2, 4.431). For n component sentences, there are $2^{(2^n)}$ sets of truth-conditions, and since each set of truth-conditions corresponds to a truth-function, there are the same number of truth-functions (the notation Wittgenstein uses to say this at T 4.27 and 4.42 belongs to probability theory).

Those truth-possibilities which make the sentence true are its *truth-grounds* (T 5.101), and accordingly we might call those which make it false its 'falsity-grounds'. To state the truth-conditions of a sentence is to state which of its truth-possibilities are its truth-grounds (those it 'agrees with'), and which are its falsity-grounds (those it 'disagrees with'). The truth-conditions of a sentence can be set out in a truth-table, thus:

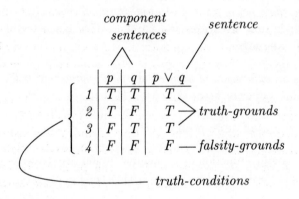

Truth-tables in the form in which they are used today were introduced in 1921 both by Wittgenstein, in the *Tractatus*, and by Emil Post (Post, 1921). The now customary presentation is a combination of the two: it uses '*T*'s and '*F*'s as in Wittgenstein's version (whereas Post used '+'s and '−'s), but it arranges the truth-possibilities in Post's manner rather than Wittgenstein's. The method, however, was not original, and is given—though not in tabular form—in Frege's *Begriffsschrift* (Frege, 1972, pp115–124). The truth-conditions of the other standard logical connectives are given (in Wittgenstein's Truth-Conditions Notation) at T 5.101.

According to the *Tractatus*, the *sense* of a sentence is given by its truth-conditions—the pattern of agreement and disagreement with its component sentences (T 4.2). (We cannot say that this is a pattern of agreement and disagreement with the facts stated by these component sentences, since if any of these component sentences is false, then the corresponding fact will not exist.) The representational content of the sentence is given by its component sentences: the rôle of the logical connectives is not to represent anything further in the world, but is to determine the pattern of agreement and disagreement which the sentence as a whole has with its component sentences. Thus the connectives are not themselves directly representational, but they do serve to determine the sense of representational sentences. This, briefly, is the theory of truth-functions, and the essential point for representational discourse is that *the logical connectives are given a rôle in representational language which does not involve their being names of anything in the world.*

Wittgenstein is now in a position to crystallise his account of representational language:

> A sentence is an expression of agreement and disagreement with truth-possibilities of elementary sentences. [T 4.4]

The thought is repeated more prominently:

> A sentence is a truth-function of elementary sentences. (An elementary sentence is a truth-function of itself.) [T 5]

And the final culmination at T 6 is the presentation of the general sentential form as:

$$[\bar{p}, \bar{\xi}, N(\bar{\xi})].$$

There is nothing odd or contentious in the Tractarian presentation of the theory of truth-functions itself, but it is worth emphasising that Wittgenstein is putting the theory to work in the service of his account of representation. The theory of truth-functions belongs by nature to Formal Logic, and is not intrinsically tied to any particular philosophical theory. However as it appears in the Tractarian *milieu*, it consorts with four very Tractarian thoughts.

1. The 'sentences' with which Wittgenstein is concerned are *representational* ones. Truth-functional statements with non-representational components might in principle be constructed, but it is no concern of the *Tractatus* to do this: Wittgenstein is concerned specifically with the explanation of representational language. A statement such as '$(a = b) \supset (b = c)$' is not at odds with the theory of truth-functions itself, but it is uninteresting to the Tractarian system, since its components, which are identity-statements, are held not to be fact-stating (see chapter 4).

2. The component statements at issue are *elementary sentences.* The Tractarian account of representation involves a reduction to the level of elementary sentences, and so it is to these that the theory of truth-functions is applied. But outside this context, the theory of truth-functions can of course be applied more freely, and there is no need in general for the component statements to be Tractarian elementary sentences.

3. The logical constants which are addressed are those of logical notation rather than those of ordinary language. The constants '&', '∨', '∼', '⊃', and '≡' (and other symbols in other dialects of the sentential calculus), for example, are counterparts of the English expressions 'and', 'or', 'not', 'if ... then ... ', and '... if and only if ... '. However, it is not clear, especially in the case of '⊃', that these symbols are truly equivalent to their ordinary language counterparts: it is not clear that ordinary language is wholly truth-functional. The *Tractatus*, though, simply ignores this issue, and assumes that we are dealing with language which can be analysed in this way.

4. The theory of truth-functions is applied in such a way as to explain the constants 'some' and 'all', as well as the other constants mentioned (see chapter 4). One might expect a separate explanation of these quantificational constants, which belong to the predicate calculus, but by its 'principle of extensionality' the Tractarian account purports to be purely truth-functional. This again is an aspect of Wittgenstein's *application* of the theory of truth-functions, rather than anything intrinsic to the theory itself.

As conceived in isolation from any special philosophical concerns, a truth-function is a many-one mapping whose domain of arguments is a set of truth-possibility-schemata (n-tuples of truth-values), and whose range of values is the (dyadic) set of truth-values. That is, its domain is $\{T, F\}^n$ for some n, and its range is the set $\{T, F\}$. The truth-function can be thought of as a set of ordered pairs: the truth-function of disjunction, for example, is the set $\{\langle\langle T, T\rangle, T\rangle, \langle\langle T, F\rangle, T\rangle, \langle\langle F, T\rangle, T\rangle, \langle\langle F, F\rangle, F\rangle\}$, and can be expressed in a table as:

$$
\begin{array}{cc|c}
T & T & T \\
T & F & T \\
F & T & T \\
F & F & F
\end{array}
$$

An operation, on the other hand, is a syntactic matter of the manipulation of symbols. It takes sentences as its *bases*, and produces a logically molecular sentence as its *result*. The operation of disjunction, for example, can be expressed as:

$$
\begin{array}{cc|c}
p & q & p \vee q
\end{array}
$$

What a truth-table does is to put an operation and a truth-function together so as to assert that the truth-values of the result of the operation and those of its bases are related in the manner determined by the truth-function. (A truth-table can therefore be right or wrong according to whether the correlation is correct with respect to the conventional meanings of the connectives.) The part of the truth-table above the horizontal line gives the operation, and that below the line gives the truth-function. Thus the truth-table for disjunction, as above, is:

$$
\begin{array}{cc|c}
p & q & p \vee q \\
\hline
T & T & T \\
T & F & T \\
F & T & T \\
F & F & F
\end{array}
$$

What we see in the *Tractatus* is this abstract theory of truth-functions put into the service of the early Wittgenstein's theory of representational language. And accordingly, the significant problems we find attach not to the theory itself, but to the philosophical aims it is made to serve.

Problems

We turn now to some of the problems associated with Wittgenstein's use of the theory of truth-functions, the first three of which are minor terminological issues.

First, Wittgenstein distinguishes between (syntactic) operation and (semantic) truth-function (T 5.25 5.251). However his use of the expression *truth-arguments* for the logically atomic components of a sentence is confusing, since it is functions rather than sentences which have 'arguments'. Wittgenstein calls 'p' and 'q' the 'truth-arguments' of '$p \& q$'. The sentences 'p' and 'q' are the bases of the operation of conjunction performed to produce the result '$p \& q$', and they are the connective-free components of '$p \& q$', but they are not straightforwardly 'arguments' of '$p \& q$'. The arguments to a truth-function are truth-values, not sentences. The only way in which component sentences can be interpreted as arguments is by regarding syntactic operations as functions from sentences and connectives to sentences, but this is not the account which Wittgenstein's gives.

Second, the statement that 'A sentence is a truth-function of elementary sentences' (T 5) is problematic. The sentence itself, for example '$p \lor q$' above, is not itself a function—rather its truth-value and the truth-values of its components are related by a function. As Frege pointed out, an equivocation in the use of 'function' is common in mathematics where

> ... the name 'function' is given sometimes to what determines the mode of dependence, or perhaps to the mode of dependence itself, and sometimes to the dependent variable. ['What is a Function', in Geach and Black, 1977]

and the mistake is made of

> ... the function with its value for an argument. [*loc cit*, p115]

Even following this equivocation, we can only say that the truth-value of a sentence is a truth-function of those of its components—we cannot say that the sentence itself is a truth-function of its components themselves. Wittgenstein's usage is at two removes from the basic notion of a function.

Third, even if all representational sentences express truth-functions of elementary sentences, the reverse is not the case. Tautologies and contradictions are truth-functional, but they are not representational: they are of the same general type as representational sentences, but they are 'degenerate', they 'say nothing', and they have no sense (T 4.461–4.462). Thus, when Wittgenstein crystalises his account of representational language at T 4.4, 5, and 6, he should really say that he intends a *logically contingent* truth-function of elementary sentences.

Fourth, Wittgenstein is infamously unpersuasive at various points where it is obviously difficult to give a purely truth-functional account of representational language. In the case of quantification, he means to explain the 'all' and 'some' of representational discourse in truth-functional terms, but he seems to end up relying on implicit quantification through the use of a variable (see chapter 4 for the conjunction/disjunction theory, and chapter 7 for the *N* operator). In the case of propositional attitudes such as belief, Wittgenstein's account is brief and unclear (T 5.54–5.5423; cf Black, *Companion*, pp298–302). And regarding the seemingly non-truth-functional nature of ordinary language constants such as 'if ... then ... ', he says nothing at all.

Fifth, Wittgenstein seems to want the theory of truth-functions to do more than just explain the rôle of the logical connectives in normal representational sentences. He wants it to perform the second rôle of explaining the *analysis* required to get from normal representational sentences to elementary sentences. Thus he states (at T 4.4 and 5, quoted above) that a sentence is a truth-function of *elementary sentences*. He is not concerned here with the relation between a normal logically molecular sentence written on a page and its logically atomic components also written on the page, but rather with the relation between a normal sentence, molecular or otherwise, and the elementary sentences into which it can be analysed.

A sentence's being logically atomic is not of course the same thing as its being elementary: for example the sentence 'Grass is green' is logically atomic, but it is certainly not in the Tractarian sense elementary. Indeed, if this were so there would be no problem in giving examples of elementary sentences—we should only need to look for those which contain no logical constants. Logical atomicity is a necessary but not sufficient condition of elementarity: if a sentence is elementary, it follows that it contains no logical constants, but the reverse is not the case. To say that a sentence contains no logical constants is not to say that it is a concatenation of Tractarian names, each of which refers—or could refer—to a Tractarian object. Therefore, the usual truth-functional analysis of a sentence of ordinary language will not yield what is required.

Nevertheless, Wittgenstein does mean to say that a normal sentence, on analysis, yields a truth-function of elementary sentences. There seems to be an element of wishful thinking here. It may indeed be so that the product of analysis is a truth-function—it might be a conjunction of elementary sentences—but this is not to say that the theory of truth-functions alone provides us with a sufficient method of analysis. The theory of truth-functions does not, so to speak, give us a method of extracting the elementary sentences. In particular, a purely truth-functional analysis does not affect the names appearing in the original sentence, but *normal sentences do not contain Tractarian elementary names*, and so more than truth-functional analysis is required to get us to elementary sentences, which do allegedly consist of elementary names.

The proposed analysis of a logically molecular sentence would actually proceed in two stages. The molecular sentence would be analysed as a truth-function of logically atomic sentences; each of these would be analysed as a truth-function of elementary sentences; and then the two levels of analysis would be resolved into one truth-function of elementary sentences. This resolution is not a problem for the theory of truth-functions, rather the problem is that much more than the theory of truth-functions is required to perform the second stage of analysis.

We are thus left with the several problems of the early Wittgenstein's concept of analysis (see chapter 2). What the theory of truth-functions actually does in the *Tractatus* is to *complement* the picture theory by explaining the rôle of the logical constants in representational sentences: it does not in addition solve the picture theory's problems.

Conclusion

The theory of truth-functions is fixed deep within the web of the Tractarian system, and so at a number of points it has been necessary to anticipate issues discussed in later chapters. Chapter 4 concerns the *Grundgedanke*, which motivates the theory of truth-functions in the context of representational language, and also leads, through the Logical Independence Thesis, discussed in chapter 5, to the thesis that logic is syntactic. This latter thesis is discussed in chapter 6, together with the other rôle of the theory of truth-functions: the provision of a 'syntactic' explanation of logical properties and relations.

Part III

INSIDE THE MIRROR

Chapter 4

The Grundgedanke

Introduction

The journey inside the great mirror is perhaps the most interesting feature of the *Tractatus*. This is the investigation of the intra-linguistic realm of what is internal to our representational systems— of what belongs not to the facts described by a system, but to the inner relations of the system itself.

In the *Tractatus* logic, probability, modality, and the subject matters, if they can properly be called that, of mathematics, scientific theory, and philosophy are all deemed to be syntactic. In each case, although it may seem that we are dealing with external facts (presumably special facts of an eternal, universal, abstract character), we are actually dealing with something intra-linguistic.

The *Tractatus* may not have a centre, but it does have a drift— the drift out of the factual world. And most of what is moved out of the factual world ends up in the syntactic division. The reader of the *Tractatus* is not assisted in seeing this, but if it is not seen, then it becomes virtually impossible to make cohesive sense out of the middle and final passages of the book. No single technical term is used to denote the intra-linguistic (and so the expression 'the syntactic' has been introduced here), the discussions of the various topics are not explicitly coordinated with one another, and the treatment of logic is comparatively long whereas the others are very brief. In particular, it is not made clear that the various discussions share a common opposition to Naïve Representationalism: in each case, something which seems to be reflected in the great mirror is held to

47

belong *inside* the mechanism of reflection.

The present chapter and chapters 5, 6, and 7 are devoted to the Tractarian treatment of logic—the *Grundgedanke*, the logical vacuity of the factual world, the syntactic nature of logic, and the consequences of these views for logical notation. The other inhabitants of the syntactic domain are discussed in chapter 8.

The *Grundgedanke* and the Picture Theory

Wittgenstein's *Grundgedanke* or 'fundamental thought' is presented in an emphatic statement which appears in the midst of his discussion of the picture theory of meaning:

> The possibility of sentences is based on the principle that objects have signs as their representatives. My fundamental thought is that the 'logical constants' are not representatives; that there can be no representatives of the *logic* of facts. [T 4.0312]

That is: the logical constants—the connectives '∨', '&', '⊃' etc., the identity sign '=', and the quantifiers '( )' and '∃'—*are not names of substantive objects in the world*.

Although Wittgenstein calls this thesis his 'fundamental thought', and gives it equally great emphasis in the *Prototractatus*, the *Notebooks*, and in his early letters to Russell, its connection with its supporting arguments, and its decisive support for the thesis that logic is syntactic, are obscured in the text of the *Tractatus*, and have remained something of a mystery. Max Black, for example, says:

> The rejection of 'logical objects' marks a climax in Wittgenstein's inquiry. It is, as he puts it, a 'fundamental thought' for him that the so-called 'logical constants' do not stand for anything in the world (4.0312b). His entire conception of logic turns on this. [*Companion*, p264]

However Black does not explain *why* the thought is fundamental, and how it relates to the picture theory; and of Wittgenstein's supporting arguments adduced below, he appeals in this context only to the first and third. Erik Stenius, in discussing the *Grundgedanke*, briefly mentions its connection with the picture theory, and some of Wittgenstein's supporting arguments, but does not explain its importance (*Exposition*, pp144–5). The aim of the present chapter and the next is to elucidate the point and consequences of the *Grundgedanke*, and to marshal its supporting arguments.

Wittgenstein went to Cambridge to study under Russell in 1911. However, a passage from Jourdain's notes from 20 April 1909 indicates that Wittgenstein had come into contact with Russell's views sometime before this date:

> Russell said that the views I gave in a reply to Wittgenstein (who had 'solved' Russell's contradiction) agree with his own. [Grattan-Guinness, 1977, p114]

Grattan-Guinness discusses the evidence and concludes that 'the legitimacy of the passage seems indisputable': Jourdain and Wittgenstein had been in contact concerning Russell's paradox, presumably by letter, before the date the passage was written, and so it seems that Wittgenstein's first contact with Russell's writings occurred as early as 1909.

At this time Russell held to a representational view of the logical constants, and so it is possible that it was then that Wittgenstein first developed his non-representational theory as a reaction. In any case, the earliest evidence of Wittgenstein's views on the logical constants is to be found in his letters to Russell from 1912 and 1913. It is clear from these early letters that Wittgenstein was greatly exercised over the problem of the sense of molecular or 'complex' sentences, and the rôle which the constants play in these. The question at issue is that of how the constants contribute to the meanings of the sentences in which they appear, and in particular whether they are names of things in the world—whether they are what Wittgenstein later called 'proxies' for 'logical objects'. Although Wittgenstein does occasionally use 'logical constant' to mean the same as 'logical object', his meaning is clear, and the question is always whether logical constants in the sentence function by being names of logical objects in the world.

> ...there are NO *logical* constants. [Cambridge, 22.6.1912; LR, p10]

What troubles me most at present, is not the apparent-variable-business, but rather the meaning of '∨', '.', '⊃' etc. This latter problem is—I think—still more fundamental and, if possible, still less recognised as a problem ... If '$p \vee q$' does not mean a complex, then heaven knows what it means!! [Hochreit, Summer 1912; LR, p13]

The 'complex problem' of the rôle of logical constants is frequently mentioned in Wittgenstein's early writings (for example LR, pp15, 16, 17; N pp13, 15, 19, 22, 27, 29, 36, 45). And in the 'Notes on Logic', Wittgenstein states what was to be his basic position:

That 'or' and 'not' etc. are not relations in the same sense as 'right' and 'left' etc., is obvious to the plain man. [NL, p101]

In the *Tractatus*, the relation which the *Grundgedanke* bears to the picture theory is emphasised by the textual arrangement. In the early 4's there appears an extended exposition of the picture theory, and the *Grundgedanke* appears towards the end of this, at 4.0312. In particular the remark immediately preceding the statement of the *Grundgedanke* is a clear statement of the picture theory:

One name stands for one thing, another for another thing, and they are combined with one another. In this way the whole group— like a *tableau vivant*—presents an elementary fact. [T 4.0311; cf N, p26]

And the first sentence of 4.0312 is a brief reiteration of the picture theory's naming principle.

In the *Notebooks* and in the *Prototractatus* the same idea is expressed, in very similar wording, and is also called the 'fundamental thought'. Here also, the *Grundgedanke* appears in the context of the picture theory, and it is made clear that molecular sentences cannot be treated as pictures, *since the constants they contain are not names* (N, p37; PT 4.01, 4.0101, 4.0102, 4.0103). If a sentence is to be a picture, then its constituents must be names of substantive objects in the world, but according to the *Grundgedanke* the logical constants are not of this type: thus the *Grundgedanke* sets a limit to the applicability of the pure picture theory of meaning.

Several years later Wittgenstein still retained the view that the logical constants are not names of relations between facts. Friedrich

Waismann records that in 1930 Wittgenstein said in conversation that:

> ... 'not', 'and ', 'or', and 'if' do not connect objects. And I still adhere to that. [WN, p74]

And in 1931, Wittgenstein wrote:

> Incidentally, when I was in Norway during the year 1913–14 I had some thoughts of my own, or so at least it seems to me now. I mean I have the impression that at that time I brought to life new movements in thinking (but perhaps I am mistaken). Whereas now I seem just to apply old ones. [CV, p20]

It was in late 1914 that Wittgenstein recorded in his Notebooks that his fundamental thought was that the logical constants are not representatives of objects in the world. Thus during the period which Wittgenstein later held to have been his most fruitful, he held the *Grundgedanke* to be fundamental.

The first point of importance about the *Grundgedanke* is that it asserts that the picture theory does not account for molecular sentences. If it is applied to such sentences, the picture theory, through its naming principle, requires that the logical constants function as names just as the other components of the sentence do. That is, on what might be called the 'Pictorial View' of the logical constants, it is required that when a molecular sentence is true, there should be in the world a fact which contains *logical* objects named by the logical constants, along with the non-logical objects named by the other components of the sentence. On this view, a logically molecular sentence depicts a logically molecular fact, just as a logically atomic sentence depicts a logically atomic fact. For example, a sentence of the form '$p \lor q$' would be true just in case the world contained a compound fact composed of the fact p, the fact q, and the logical object of disjunction. However, as Wittgenstein shows in a number of arguments, this cannot be the case. If we try to apply the picture theory to a logical constant it is treated as a logical name, naming a logical object, just as the non-logical names are treated as the names of non-logical objects, and this is mistaken. In the context of the *Tractatus*, it is therefore with regard to the picture theory's naming thesis (rather than the structural isomorphism thesis) that the *Grundgedanke* arises.

Logical constants contribute to the senses of the sentences in which they appear. The naïve assumption is that they serve as relational expressions to express relations between facts in the world. For instance, when we say something of the form '$p \lor q$' we mean that two facts p and q in the world are connected by the relation of disjunction; and when we say '$r \supset (p \lor q)$' we mean that the fact r is related by material implication to the disjunctive fact $p \lor q$ etc. The Pictorial View of the constants has both a linguistic and an ontological side: on the linguistic side it classifies the constants as names, and, more importantly, on the ontological side it posits the existence of logical objects. To assert the existence of such logical objects is to assert the existence of molecular facts—compound facts made up of atomic facts and logical objects—so according to the Pictorial View, there would be disjunctive facts, materially implicative facts etc., just as there are logically atomic facts. Wittgenstein argues in detail against this view, and the conclusion of his three main lines of argument is that the Pictorial View is false: the world does not contain logical objects, and consequently it does not contain molecular facts. All facts are logically atomic, and none contain logical objects.

It is worth emphasising that this is a substantive thesis, and is not a matter of definition. The Tractarian elementary facts (*Sachverhalte*) are defined as configurations of objects, and Wittgenstein's thesis in the *Grundgedanke* is that none of these objects is 'logical'. If *Sachverhalt* is translated as 'atomic fact', this point is obscured, since the word 'atomic' suggests both ontological and logical simplicity, and it then seems to be a matter of definition that *Sachverhalte* are logically atomic.

Those of Wittgenstein's arguments in support of the *Grundgedanke* which concern the logical connectives appear in the 4.4's and the 5.4's in the *Tractatus*, and those which concern the quantifiers and the identity sign appear mostly in the 5.5's. (The Tractarian numbering system does not serve its purpose here: the *Grundgedanke* is given in 4.0312, which in the numbering system has no special connection with the 4.4's, 5.4's, and 5.5's, where its supporting arguments appear.) The remarks concerning the connectives can be grouped into three arguments: (1) the Argument from Equivalence, (2) the Argument from Brackets, and (3) the Argument from Alternative Notation, and these will now be considered in turn.

The Argument from Equivalence

The relation between the Argument from Equivalence and the *Grundgedanke* is not perfectly linear: this argument is used in support of the *Grundgedanke*, which opens the way for the truth-functional account of the connectives, but the Argument from Equivalence appeals to a principle which belongs to the theory of truth-functions—the principle that sentences which have the same truth-conditions have the same sense. And it is presumably for this reason that the argument is presented in the 5's, once the theory of truth-functions has been worked out. The argument runs as follows:

A sentence is a truth-function of elementary sentences. [T 5]

At this point it becomes manifest that there are no 'logical objects' or 'logical constants' (in Frege's and Russell's sense). [T 5.4]

The reason is that the results of truth-operations on truth-functions are always identical whenever they are one and the same truth-function of elementary sentences. [T 5.41]

It is self-evident that ∨, ⊃ etc. are not relations in the sense in which right and left etc. are relations. The interdefinability of Frege's and Russell's 'primitive signs' of logic is enough to show that they are not primitive signs, still less signs for relations. [T 5.42; cf NL, p101]

The general point is that sentences which have the same truth-conditions are equivalent—they have the same sense and say the same thing—and this is so even when they use different logical constants. For example, '$p \supset q$' and '$\sim p \vee q$' are identical in truth-conditions, and so they say the same thing, although the first uses only '⊃' while the second uses '∼' and '∨'. Thus, if the Pictorial View were correct, these two sentences would differ in what they depicted, since their different logical constants would refer to different logical objects. The sentence '$p \supset q$' would depict a compound fact comprising the positive facts p and q and the relation of material implication. The sentence '$\sim p \vee q$' would depict a compound fact comprising the negative fact $\sim p$, the positive fact q, and the relation of disjunction. But the two sentences are equivalent, and so cannot differ in what they say.

The logical constants are interdefinable: any sentence containing a given constant can be reformulated so that it contains others instead, without affecting its truth-conditions—without affecting its sense. For example, any sentence of the form '$p \equiv q$' can be reformulated as '$(p \supset q) \,\&\, (q \supset p)$', so dispensing with '$\equiv$'. Likewise, any sentence of the form '$p \vee q$' can be reformulated to have the form '$\sim(\sim p \,\&\, \sim q)$', letting '$\sim$' and '$\&$' do the job of '$\vee$'. If logical constants referred to logical objects, it would surely matter that some are mentioned in one sentence while others are mentioned in another; but the only difference is notational, and sense is preserved.

Another point concerning equivalence is made in 5.43.

> Even at first sight is seems scarcely credible that there should follow from one fact p infinitely many *others*, namely $\sim\sim p$, $\sim\sim\sim\sim p$, etc. [T 5.43][1]

Wittgenstein's use of quotation marks to differentiate use and mention is scrupulous, and here he is referring to the putative facts $\sim\sim p$ and $\sim\sim\sim\sim p$, rather than to sentences which depict them, and accordingly quotation marks are not used. The word 'others' is emphasised since he is considering the objectionable consequence of the Pictorial View that one fact should as a matter of logic give rise to an infinity of other facts. In generating this infinity, Wittgenstein appeals to the law of double negation, but it can be generated in other ways. The idempotence of conjunction gives the same result: 'p' = '$p \,\&\, p$', so on the Pictorial View, the fact p entails the fact $p \,\&\, p$, which in turn entails the fact $p \,\&\, p \,\&\, p$ etc. Likewise the idempotence of disjunction, 'q' = 'q $\vee$ q', gives the result that the fact q entails the fact $q \vee q$, which entails the fact $q \vee q \vee q$ etc. And there is no need to use only one constant: less neat and predictable equivalences are easily produced using several. The point is that it is scarcely credible that one fact should give rise to a multitude of others—these would all have to obtain in the world. It is scarcely credible that since the world contains one fact, it also contains an infinity of others (and that these others should be different, and yet equivalent).

Not only can one constant be replaced by others, but in the case of negation constants can be removed without being replaced, and

---

[1]The logical relation involved is not just that of logical consequence—'follow from'—but that of equivalence.

sense is still preserved. This is the point being made when Wittgenstein says that 'operations can vanish'.

> With the logical constants one need never ask whether they exist, for they can even *vanish*! [N, p19]

> An operation can vanish (for example, negation in '$\sim\sim p$' : $\sim\sim p = p$). [T 5.254]

> And if there were an object called '$\sim$', it would follow that '$\sim p$' said something different from what 'p' said, just because the one sentence would then be about—and the other would not. [T 5.44]

Strictly speaking, what vanishes is an operator—a constant—rather than an operation. The logical principle is just the commonplace law of double negation, but Wittgenstein notices the significance which this has for the status of logical constants. Of two synonymous sentences, one uses '$\sim$' twice, but the other uses it not at all; so clearly they cannot be *about* an object referred to by '$\sim$'.

Wittgenstein restricts his point to the 'vanishing' of the negation operator, but it can be generalised without difficulty to other cases. For example, it is perhaps even more persuasive that the same is true of '$((p \,\&\, \sim p) \equiv p) \supset (p \lor p)$' and '$p$'. The two have the same truth-conditions yet the first uses the constants '$\&$', '$\sim$', '$\equiv$', '$\supset$', and '$\lor$', while the second uses none at all. Thus, although the first sentence might appear through its use of logical constants to refer to various logical objects, this cannot be the case, since the second sentence is equivalent to it and uses none at all. A similar point is made in the Argument from Alternative Notation.

In summary, three sub-arguments can be distinguished in the Argument from Equivalence, and these show that the Pictorial View with its realism of logical objects (*a*) implies that equivalent sentences depict *different* facts, which they do not, (*b*) implies that the existence of one fact necessitates the existence of an infinity of other facts, and (*c*) cannot make sense of the 'vanishing' of constants, that is of pairs of equivalent sentences of which one contains constants and the other does not.

The Argument from Brackets

The Argument from Brackets, which appears both in the *Notebooks* and in the *Tractatus*, makes the Pictorial View seem comical.

> Although it seems unimportant, it is in fact significant that the pseudo-relations of logic, such as ∨ and ⊃, need brackets—unlike real relations ... And surely no one is going to believe that brackets have an independent meaning. [T 5.461; cf MN1 p116–7]

This obscure remark is comprehensible when seen as an attack on the view that the written molecular sentence is a picture, each of whose symbols functions as the *name* of an object in the fact depicted. Thus, just as the logical constants would on this interpretation be names of objects, so by the same reasoning the parentheses would also be names of objects, which is absurd. As it is stated, the remark confuses the brackets in the sentence with their suggested referents in the fact depicted. What is significant is that in the written sentence the pseudo-relational-expressions such as '∨' and '⊃' need the brackets '(' and ')' to indicate their scope. On the Pictorial View, this implies that in the fact depicted in the world the logical objects (the 'pseudo-relations of logic such as ∨ and ⊃') are accompanied by the objects named by the brackets: but real, genuine relations are not like this—they are not accompanied in this way. It is hard to believe that, for example, '$p \vee (p \supset q)$' depicts a compound fact comprising p, q, and the relations of material implication and disjunction; but to believe that this compound fact also incorporates the referents of '(' and ')' is harder still.

A similar point (this time concerning horizontal and vertical lines) arises in the Argument from Alternative Notation, discussed below, where it is pointed out that these lines in Tabular Notation do not refer to objects in the world.

However, this is not a conclusive argument against logical objects, since it is sometimes necessary to use brackets in sentences describing real, legitimate relations. For example, if we say something of the form 'A brings it about that (B brings it about that C)', the relation is real enough, but we need brackets to express what we mean. The relational expression is not associative: the sentence is not equivalent to '(A brings it about that B) brings it about that C', and so the brackets cannot be left implicit, and without any brackets the sentence is meaningless or at least ambiguous. Thus, we cannot in general infer from the necessity of using brackets that no real relation is referred to, and so the necessity of using brackets in logical notation does not itself imply that the logical constants do not name substantive logical objects.

If this remark were presented as an autonomous argument against logical objects, it could therefore be disregarded. But it seems fairer to treat T 5.461 as a sketch of the subject from one particular angle, in the manner described later in the preface to the *Philosophical Investigations*. What makes the remark obscure is its unstated context—namely, the question of the viability of the Pictorial View of logical constants. In this context the point of the remark is clear: the very same assumptions—those of the Pictorial View—which lead to the treatment of logical constants as names of objects in the world, also lead to the treatment of the brackets in molecular sentences as names of objects in the world; and this latter consequence, which is even more evidently wrong than the former, allows us to refute by *reductio* the assumptions which lead to it. On the Pictorial View, all the elements in a molecular sentence are names, and this applies to the brackets as well as to the logical constants in the sentence. By discrediting the view that brackets are names, Wittgenstein discredits the Pictorial View. Thus with regard to the logical constants, the Argument from Brackets is indirect: its immediate target is the Pictorial View, which is the reason we might have for believing in logical objects.

It could still be maintained, however, that room is left for the view that all elements in a sentence *except* the brackets are names, and so independent proof is needed of the falsity of the Pictorial View regarding the constants. Hence we must look to the other arguments for more direct support for the *Grundgedanke*.

The Argument from Alternative Notation

The Argument from Alternative Notation is a close relative of the Argument from Equivalence. In the Argument from Equivalence, the point is made that within Russellian notation the connectives can 'vanish' while preserving sense: that is, one sentence in Rus-

sellian notation which contains connectives may be equivalent to
another sentence in Russellian notation which does not. In the Argument from Alternative Notation the related point is made that
the connectives can be made to vanish by moving outside Russellian notation: what is expressed by any sentence of the sentential
calculus written in Russellian notation can equally be expressed by
sentences in what I shall call Wittgenstein's 'Tabular Notation' and
'Truth Conditions-Notation', and the point is that in these notations
nothing appears which might be thought to be the name of a logical
object. The argument appears in the 4.4's:

> The sign that results from correlating the mark 'T' with truth-possibilities is a sentential sign. [T 4.44]

> It is clear that a complex of the signs 'T' and 'F' has no object (or complex of objects) corresponding to it, just as there is
> none corresponding to the horizontal and vertical lines or to the
> brackets.—There are no 'logical objects'. Of course the same applies to all signs that express what the schemata of 'T's and 'F's
> express. [T 4.441]

> For example, the following is a sentential sign:

'p	q	'
T	T	T
F	T	T
T	F	
F	F	T

> ... If the order of the truth-possibilities in a schema is fixed once
> and for all by a combinatory rule, then the last column by itself
> will be an expression of the truth-conditions. If we now write this
> column as a row, the sentential sign will become

$$'(TT - T)(p, q)'$$

> or more explicitly

$$'(TTFT)(p, q)'.$$

(The number of places in the left-hand pair of brackets is determined by the number of terms in the right-hand pair.) [T 4.442]

The sentence in Tabular Notation and that in Truth Conditions
Notation are equivalent, and both express material implication: they
mean the same as '$p \supset q$'. According to present convention, we
would add an 'F' in the third row, instead of leaving a space, and
we would order the truth-possibilities in Post's manner. Adopting
these changes, '$p \lor q$' and '$p \equiv q$', for example, are expressed as follows:

Russellian Notation	*Tabular Notation*			*Truth Conditions Notation*

	p	q		
	T	T	T	
$p \lor q$	T	F	T	*(TTTF)(p, q)*
	F	T	T	
	F	F	F	

	p	q		
	T	T	T	
$p \equiv q$	T	F	F	*(TFFT)(p, q)*.
	F	T	F	
	F	F	T	

As in the Argument from Equivalence, the point is that we can
say just the same as we do in Russellian notation without using
anything which could be thought to be the name of a logical object,
and so it follows that even when we might appear to be referring to
logical objects, we are not actually doing so.

In Russellian notation the connectives are inscribed as one would
naturally inscribe relational operators, and this suggests that the
connectives are names for relational logical objects. This is not to
say that Russellian notation is defective as a notation, but rather
that it can be erroneously interpreted so as to suggest a philosophical fallacy. Wittgenstein's Tabular and Truth Conditions notations
are proposed, not as alternatives for general use, but in order to
show that this Pictorial View of the connectives is false. These notations contain no elements which could be thought to name logical

objects, and since sentences in this notation do not involve reference
to logical objects it follows that equivalent sentences in Russellian
notation do not do so either. (When Wittgenstein mentions brackets in T 4.441 the reference is not properly to his Tabular Notation,
since this contains no brackets, but is to Russellian notation and
reiterates the point made in the Argument from Brackets.)

The natural persuasiveness of realism about logical objects is a
product of the notation we commonly use, since this gives a grammatical rôle to its logical connectives analogous to that given to
signs for genuine relations. Hence the construction of alternative
notations which do not use logical connectives, but which can express what Russellian notation expresses, removes this persuasiveness. And most importantly, since a sentence in one of these notations evidently involves no reference to logical objects, it follows
that any synonymous sentence, in whatever notation, also involves
no reference to logical objects.

Three Further Arguments

In addition to the arguments given by Wittgenstein, the following
three arguments can be directed against the Pictorial View of logical
connectives.

Ramsey's Argument

Frank Ramsey, who had assisted in the translation of the *Tractatus*
for its first publication in English, visited Wittgenstein in Puchberg
in Austria in 1923 and 1924, where Wittgenstein was at the time
a school teacher; and in a letter to his mother Ramsey gives an
illuminating account of his meetings with Wittgenstein (LO, pp77–
78). Ramsey's visit of 1923 lasted a fortnight, and each day Wittgenstein spent several hours with him explaining the *Tractatus* (LO,
p77). In the paper 'Facts and Propositions' written in 1927, Ramsey
advances arguments against logical objects, and although Wittgenstein is not mentioned by name, these arguments are similar to some
of those in the *Tractatus*, and are evidently the product of Wittgenstein's influence (Ramsey, *Foundations*, pp40–57).

Ramsey notes that an account of sentences 'by means of names
alone' has difficulty with molecular sentences, since it indicates a re-

alist view of logical objects, which implies that 'every proposition is ultimately affirmative', that is, every proposition simply states that a fact obtains in the world. From this the unpalatable consequence follows that logical truths depict 'necessary facts'. Ramsey approaches Wittgenstein's Argument from Equivalence from a slightly different angle by saying that the conclusion of a formal inference cannot be 'something new': the point is essentially that if one proposition is equivalent to another, then it cannot say something new—it is, as Ramsey says, 'the same fact expressed by other words'.

Ramsey also suggests a notational innovation, in an argument akin to Wittgenstein's argument from Tabular Notation. The suggestion is that instead of expressing negation by an operator such as '∼', we do so by inverting the sentence: the result is that double negation is self cancelling, and we do not have equivalences through the law of double negation. Although Ramsey notes that this argument shows that some equivalents can be eliminated, he does not explicitly draw the important interim conclusion that the possibility of such notation shows that syntactically different but logically equivalent sentences do not concern different logical objects. Another restriction in Ramsey's argument is that it only concerns negation: it is akin to the Argument from Alternative Notation but is restricted to negation in the point that it makes. The conclusion he draws, though, is that ' "not" cannot be a name'.

The Argument from Assimilation

A further reason for rejecting the Pictorial View of the logical constants is that is has the consequence that all the dyadic connectives are assimilated to conjunction. On the Pictorial View, for any logical connective $\otimes$, if '$p \otimes q$' is true this is so because the world contains the fact p, the fact q, and the relational logical object $\otimes$ connecting these two facts. In order that the relation $\otimes$ be instantiated in this particular case, the world must contain p and q: the relation must have relata. The Pictorial View treats molecular sentences in the same way as it treats atomic sentences: just as the truth of 'Peter is taller than Paul' requires the existence in the world of the entity Peter, the entity Paul, and the relation is-taller-then connecting them; so, on this view, the truth of '$p \lor q$' requires the existence in the world of the fact p, the fact q, and the relation of disjunction connecting these. The Pictorial View requires that in order that '$p \otimes q$' be true, 'p' and 'q' must both be true, which is evidently mistaken. The result of this is that *all the dyadic connectives have the truth-conditions of conjunction*: in the case of '$p \,\&\, q$' it is correct that the compound sentence is true if and only if both of its components are. But with the other dyadic connectives this is not so: in the case of disjunction, for example, '$p \vee q$' is true when both 'p' and 'q' are true, and when only one of them is true, but false when neither component is true. In the case of material implication, '$p \supset q$' is true when both 'p' and 'q' are true, when neither are true, and when 'p' is false and 'q' is true, but not when 'p' is true and 'q' is false, and so on.

It might be suggested in defence that logical objects connect negative facts as well as positive ones, so that, for example, if our compound sentence is '$p \vee q$', and 'p' is true while 'q' is false, then in the world the fact p is connected by the logical object of disjunction with the negative fact *not-q*. But this is not what the compound sentence says: it disjoins two positive things, and on the Pictorial View this means that it expresses a disjunction in the world between two positive facts. The expression 'q' in '$p \vee q$' gives no indication that its referent might be a negative fact.

The Argument from Logical Privilege

Finally, the Pictorial View also has the consequence that some logical relations can obtain in the world while others cannot. If there were logical objects then there would be molecular facts, and if there were molecular facts, then there would be logical relations between these: for example the molecular fact $p \,\&\, q$ would have as a logical consequence the molecular fact $p \vee q$ (see chapter 5). However, in the case of inconsistency between a fact A and a fact B, it would be required that both A and B exist in the world, and that the relation of inconsistency obtain between them. But this would be impossible, since if the two facts were 'inconsistent' then they could not both exist at once. Thus although, on this account, some logical relations such as logical consequence, logical equivalence, and subcontrariety could obtain between facts in the world, others such as inconsistency and proper contradiction could not. And surely any account of the logical relations must treat them all equally: it would be absurd to

suggest that some are privileged in being instantiated in the world
while others are not.

Quantification

The arguments considered so far have been those which Wittgenstein
explicitly directs against the Pictorial View of the logical constants,
together with an argument of Ramsey's and two supplementary arguments. These all concern the logical connectives '~', '⊃', '∨', '≡'
etc., rather than the remaining constants of the predicate calculus—
the quantifiers and the identity sign—which also need to be considered.

The semantics of the quantifiers can be a serious matter, as
emerges in Homer's *Odyssey* when Odysseus gives his name as 'Nobody' in order to trick Polyphemos the Cyclops. Odysseus addresses
the Cyclops and says:

> Nobody is my name. My father and mother call me Nobody, as
> do all my friends.

Odysseus then tries to kill Polyphemos, in order to avoid being eaten
by him, and when the other Cyclopes hear Polyphemos' cries and
ask what is the matter he replies:

> Oh my good friends, Nobody's treachery is killing me.

On hearing this, the other Cyclopes naturally conclude that Polyphemos does not need help, and answer:

> Well then, if Nobody is assaulting you in your solitude, you must
> be sick [*Odyssey*, Book 9, 366–414]

And as a result Odysseus is able to make his escape.

The point, of course, is that 'Nobody' is not the name of an
entity (or person), and that nonsense results if we treat it as such.
Although Wittgenstein does not emphasise through the Tractarian
numbering system, or through his turn of phrase, that his remarks on
the quantifiers and the identity-sign are in accord with the *Grundgedanke*, his view is likewise that these are not names of objects. An
Argument from Equivalence concerning the 'vanishing' of quantifiers
appears at T 5.411, and the basic Tractarian thought on generality
appears in the 4's:

It immediately strikes one as probable that the introduction of
elementary sentences gives the basis for understanding all other
kinds of sentence. Indeed the understanding of general sentences
palpably depends on the understanding of elementary sentences.
[T 4.411]

The details given in the *Tractatus* of how this is to be achieved are
hard to follow, and H.O. Mounce's view is that they are confused
(*Introduction*, p67). G. E. Moore records that Wittgenstein later
said that this view at the time of the *Tractatus* had been that universally quantified statements are covert conjunctions, and that exis-
tentially quantified statements are covert disjunctions (MN2, pp297–
299). This account of Wittgenstein's early view of quantification is
further corroborated by his later statement that his 'former view
of generality' interpreted an existential sentence so that it 'behaves
like a logical sum' (*Philosophical Grammar*, p268). (His view by this
time was that there is no single unitary concept of *all* or *some* [cf
AN, pp68–9].) When we look to the *Tractatus*, however, we do not
find a straightforward statement of this interpretation of quantification. This is in part due to the fact that the relevant passages, in
the 5.52's, are concerned with a further issue—that of using the N
operator notation to formulate general sentences (see chapter 7).

In any case, the point for the *Grundgedanke* is that the conjunc-
tion/disjunction theory implies a non-representational account of the
quantifiers. Conjunction, as already established, is not a logical object, and so if universal quantification is explained entirely in terms
of conjunction, this too will not involve a logical object. Likewise,
disjunction is not a logical object, and so if existential quantification
is covert disjunction, then this does not involve a logical object either. Thus '( )' and '∃' are not names, proxies, or representatives of
objects in the world, and quantified sentences are not true in virtue
of their representing 'quantified' facts containing quantificational objects. The sentence 'Some men are French' is true, not because it
depicts a quantificational fact composed of the objects *some, men,*
and *French*, but rather because the disjunctive sentence 'Pierre is
French ∨ Jack is French ∨ Indra is French ∨ ...' is true. And the
sentence 'All Frenchmen drink' is true because on analysis it yields
the true sentence 'Pierre drinks & Jean-Paul drinks & Sebastian
drinks & ...'. In one remark Wittgenstein says:

If the objects are given, then *all* objects are thereby also given. If

the elementary sentences are given, then *all* elementary sentences
are thereby also given. [T 5.524]

This may in part be a play on the word 'all': there are no quantificational objects in addition to the others, and similarly there are
no quantificational elementary sentences over and above the others. Extra all-objects and all-elementary-sentences are dismissed. It
might be added to this that if the elementary facts are given, then *all*
elementary facts are thereby also given. The pun cannot be made to
work with 'some', and so is restricted to 'all', but the same point can
be made here. (In N, p76, the point is made in such a way that the
pun is more obvious. For another, rather masterful, play on words,
see T 5.143.)

Thus if the conjunction/disjunction view of quantification is ac-
cepted, the quantifiers join the connectives and their attendant brackets: they are not names of objects, and sentences containing them
do not depict quantificational facts in the world.

Identity

In the 5.53's Wittgenstein rejects the idea that the identity-sign '='
is the name of an object, or a relation obtaining between things in
the world:

> It is self-evident that identity is not a relation between objects.
> [T 5.5301]

The remark with the greatest numerical 'stress' is:

> Identity of the object I express by identity of the sign and not
> by means of a sign of identity. Difference of objects I express by
> difference of signs. [T 5.53]

And as a comment on this he says:

> The identity-sign, therefore, is not an essential constituent of a
> conceptual notation. [T 5.533]

The essential idea is to insist on using a language in which there are no co-referential names. There will then be no need for a special *sign* to indicate identity or difference: sameness or difference of names will do.

The identity-sign has the same *grammatical* rôle as a relational expression: we say '$A = B$' just as we say 'A eats B', and this may give the impression that the identity-sign is, like its grammatical cognates, the name of a relation obtaining between entities in the world. Against this view, Wittgenstein gives a dispensability-argument akin to those given against the Pictorial View of the connectives in the Argument from Equivalence and the Argument from Alternative Notation. By introducing a new notation free of co-referential expressions we can dispense with the identity-sign altogether. In such a notation there is no quasi-relational identity-sign, and since we can nevertheless convey the *same* information about the world, it follows that the identity-sign in our usual notation does not name anything in the world either.

In the new notation there is no sign which even seems to refer to a relation of identity holding between entities in the world, and since *nothing is lost*, we can infer that when using the identity-sign we were not referring to a real relation of identity in the first place. The point is not really that we all *should* communicate in such a language, but rather that we *could*, without losing expressive power. Just as the connectives can be dispensed with by using Tabular Notation, or in some cases by making them 'vanish', so here the identity-sign can be dispensed with by adopting Wittgenstein's proposal. In each case what is dispensed with is a seemingly referential expression: in the case of the connectives we can dispense with the apparently referential signs '$\lor$', '$\sim$', '$\&$' etc., and in the case of the identity-sign we can dispense with '$=$'. And in both cases, since sentences which seem to state that relations hold in the world can be replaced by sentences which do not do this, it emerges that reference to such relations is merely an illusion generated by an accident of grammar.

It might be objected with regard to definite descriptions that the elimination of the identity sign would diminish the expressive power of a language. We commonly make statements of the form 'The $F = a$', for example, 'The capital city of Austria *is* Vienna', and with the elimination of the identity sign we should still want to be able to express such thoughts.

However the problem of formulating equivalent statements in an identity-free notation can be solved in two stages, first by translating definite descriptions along the lines suggested in Russell's Theory of Descriptions (Russell, 1905), and second by using Wittgenstein's rule for variables.

By the first procedure we translate 'The $F = a$' into 'There is exactly one x such that $F(x)$, and $F(a)$'. We could represent this latter as '$(\exists x)[F(x)\&(y)[F(y)\supset y = x]]$', but here we have introduced the identity sign again, which defeats our objective.

However, Wittgenstein's treatment of variables in his proposed language is analogous to his treatment of names, and this solves the problem. The rule is introduced in T 5.532 and 5.5321, and the idea, as Black puts it, is that 'visibly different variables shall be treated *differently* for purposes of instantiation—so that, for example, $R(x,y)$ shall not be permitted to have $R(a,a)$ as a substitution instance' (*Companion*, p293). Wittgenstein gives a number of examples of identity statements in Russellian notation reformulated according to this rule, one of which is:

And the sentence '*Only* one x satisfies $f()$', will read
'$(\exists x).fx \;:\; \sim(\exists x,y).fx.fy$'. [T 5.5321]

Wittgenstein's '*only* one' means 'exactly one': there is something which is f, but it is not the case that there are two *different* things which are f. Thus 'The $F = a$' can be translated, through these two stages, to '$(\exists x).Fx \;\&\; \sim(\exists x,y).Fx.Fy \;\&\; F(a)$'. This says the same as our first formulation, but does not use the identity sign, and so the problem is solved.

Several years later Wittgenstein still retained this account of identity, as indicated in the following records of his conversations and lectures of 1930, 1930–31, and 1934–35 respectively.

We see that identity is a mere rule dealing with signs from the fact that it disappears as soon as we use a language which represents every object by means of *one* sign. [No. 6 in Waismann's 'Theses' in WN, p243]

... horse = quadruped genus equus is about the type-sign horse. [LN, p113]

Russell's notation gives rise to puzzlement because it makes identity appear to be a relation between two things . . . What is bad
about Russell's notation is that it leads one to think there is such
a proposition as $x = y$, or $x = x$. One can introduce a notation in
which the identity sign Russell used can be abolished. [AN, p146;
cf p207]

Identity statements are non-representational: the identity-sign
'=' is not the name of an object in the world, and so identity sentences are not about the world, they are not part of 'natural science',
they 'say' nothing, they do not have 'sense' etc. Thus there are no
identity facts, and there can be no representational sentences stating
identities. Identity is a creature not of the world, but of language,
which is after all *prima facie* reasonable, since nobody has ever found
two objects in the world which are truly identical.

However, Wittgenstein does seem to take a stronger view concerning the identity-sign than he does concerning the logical connectives, since he asserts that identity statements are nonsense:

Roughly speaking, to say of *two* things that they are identical is
nonsense, and to say of *one* thing that it is identical with itself is
to say nothing at all. [T 5.5303]

And he says that in a 'correct conceptual notation' such 'pseudo-
sentences . . . cannot even be written down' (T 5.534). However, his
case is not quite as condemnatory as he suggests: what is wrong is to
think that identity statements 'say' something about the world, but
if we interpret them as being about signs, then they are no longer inadmissible. As an alternative notational innovation we could simply
insist that the terms of an identity sentence be enclosed in quotation marks, and we could interpret the identity-sign as meaning 'is
co-referential with'. Thus instead of '$a = b$' we could write ' "a" =
"b" ', and instead of interpreting this as meaning that the relation
of identity holds between a and b in the world, we should interpret
it as meaning that 'a' and 'b' are co-referential. What Wittgenstein's discussion really indicates is not that the identity-sign itself
is inadmissible, but that the representational interpretation of identity statements, invited by their grammatical form in the notation
normally used, is wrong.

Russell's Views

In arguing that the logical constants are not names of objects in the world, Wittgenstein was arguing against a view entertained by Russell at the time he and Wittgenstein met. Russell however expressed uncertainty over this view, and it would be unfair to say that he held to it as a dogma. In 1903 Russell had written:

> The discussion of indefinables—which forms the chief part of philosophical logic—is the endeavour to see clearly, and to make others see clearly, the entities concerned, in order that the mind may have the kind of acquaintance with them which it has with redness or the taste of a pineapple. Where, as in the present case, the indefinables are obtained primarily as the necessary residue in a process of analysis, it is often easier to know that there must be such entities than actually to perceive them; there is a process analogous to that which resulted in the discovery of Neptune, with the difference that the final stage—the search with a mental telescope for the entity which has been inferred—is often the most difficult part of the undertaking. [*Principles of Mathematics*, Preface, p xv]

By 'indefinables', Russell means the logical constants (see *op cit*, p11, p112), though he included among these the 'notion of a relation' and 'the notion of a term to a class of which it is a member' (*op cit*, p3). It seems, however, that Wittgenstein convinced Russell very quickly that the realist view of logical objects was mistaken. Wittgenstein and Russell first met in October 1911, and in the Lowell Lectures delivered in Boston in April 1914, Russell said:

> 'Logical constants', in short, are not entities; the words expressing them are not names . . . This fact has a very important bearing on all logic and philosophy, since it shows how they differ from the special sciences. [*Our Knowledge of the External World*, p213]

On this page a footnote appears, referring to the *Tractatus*; and in the preface to the book Russell acknowledges Wittgenstein's general influence on his thought.

In the 'Theory of Knowledge', which was written in 1914 but due to Wittgenstein's criticisms was not published during Russell's lifetime, Russell wrote:

It would seem that logical objects cannot be regarded as 'entities', and that, therefore, what we call 'acquaintance' with them cannot really be a dual relation. ['Theory of Knowledge', vol. 7, p97]

Russell, unlike Wittgenstein, was concerned with the epistemological issues connected with logic, and hence he mentions that since there are no logical objects it cannot be the case that we have acquaintance with such things. However, two' pages later he again expresses uncertainty:

Such words as *or, not, all, some*, plainly involve logical notions; and since we can use such words intelligently, we must be acquainted with the logical objects involved. But the difficulty of isolation is very great, and I do not know what the logical objects involved really are. [*op cit*, p99]

Later, in 1937, Russell expressed full agreement with Wittgenstein's anti-realism concerning logical objects:

. . . not even the most ardent Platonist would suppose that the perfect 'or' is laid up in heaven, and that the 'or's' here on earth are imperfect copies of the celestial archetype. [*Principles of Mathematics*, 2nd ed., p ix]

Logical constants, therefore, if we are to be able to say anything definite about them, must be regarded as part of the language, not as part of what the language speaks about. In this way logic becomes much more linguistic than I believed it to be at the time when I wrote the 'Principles'. It will still be true that no constants except the logical constants occur in the verbal or symbolic expression of logical propositions, but it will not be true that these logical constants are the names of objects, as 'Socrates' is intended to be. [*op cit*, p xii]

Here the view Russell rejects is platonic, rather than empirical, realism concerning logical objects, but the conclusion he draws is just the one Wittgenstein drew, namely, that logic belongs to language. However, this conclusion does not follow immediately, and requires an intermediate argument, discussed in chapter 5, which neither Wittgenstein nor Russell supplies.

Thus, although Russell at one time entertained the view that the logical constants are names of logical objects, he came to hold to the doctrine expressed in Wittgenstein's *Grundgedanke* that there are no logical objects in the world, and that the logical constants are not names of such entities. (See also Chadwick, 1927 for a case in favour of logical objects.)

Summary

Wittgenstein's negative view of the logical constants, which he expressed in the *Tractatus* and which he later retained, was that these are not names of substantive entities in the world. The Pictorial View of the constants is dismissed, and it is denied that the world contains 'logical objects' which are constituents of facts. Language contains both logically atomic and logically molecular sentences, but the world contains only logically atomic facts. This is a substantive thesis rather than a matter of definition: Wittgenstein's ontologically basic elementary facts (*Sachverhalte*) are defined as configurations of objects, but the thesis that none of these objects is 'logical' is separately expressed and established by the *Grundgedanke* and its supporting arguments.

Wittgenstein's arguments from Equivalence, Brackets, and Alternative Notation, which concern the logical connectives '$\sim$', '$\vee$', '$\supset$' etc., and his arguments concerning the quantifiers and the identity-sign, have been discussed (and his views on modality are considered chapter 8). These arguments coalesce—if his view on the quantifiers is taken to be the conjunction/disjunction theory —to give a single, coherent, non-representational view of the constants, as expressed in the *Grundgedanke*: '$\sim$', '$\supset$', '$\vee$', '$.$', '$\equiv$', '$\exists$', '$()$', and '$=$' are not names of objects, and do not have referents which are relations between facts or which are constituents of molecular facts. An argument of Ramsey's and two further arguments advanced above also lead to the same conclusion.

As already mentioned, Wittgenstein's arguments to this conclusion do not rely on the particular ontology put forward in the *Tractatus*. In the *Tractatus*, the entities which make up facts are 'objects', and so the arguments are directed against 'logical objects'; but Wittgenstein's arguments could equally be applied without assuming the correctness of this ontology.

With regard to the importance of Wittgenstein's *Grundgedanke*, three main points emerge.

First, the denial that the logical constants are names of worldly objects creates the need for an alternative explanation of their rôle in the meanings of sentences, and this is provided by the theory of truth-functions.

Second, as related in the following chapter, a direct consequence of the *Grundgedanke* is the Logical Independence Thesis which, together with the truth-functional analysis of logical properties and relations, is instrumental in establishing that logic is syntactic.

Third, the *Grundgedanke* provides a paradigmatic case of Wittgenstein's metaphilosophical views (see chapter 8). The *Tractatus* assigns philosophical discourse to the non-representational category: it concerns not the world of facts, but language, and one task assigned to it is the rectification of confusions engendered by language's superficial grammatical forms. One such confusion arises from the Fallacy of Grammatical Analogy—the error of taking expressions which are similar in their grammatical rôles to be similar in what they signify. The logical constants are an exemplary case of this: they play the same grammatical rôle as genuine relational expressions such as 'eats', 'owns', and 'is longer than', and this invites the misinterpretation that they likewise signify relations holding between things in the world. But, as Wittgenstein's discussion shows, this is not the case. However, Wittgenstein's view incorporates two interconnected theses—the linguistic thesis that the constants are not names, and the ontological thesis that the world does not contain logical objects. The latter thesis concerns the world of facts and is not simply an assertion about language; and so it does not fit with the view that the subject of philosophical investigation is purely syntactic.

Chapter 5

The Logical Independence Thesis

The thesis that facts in the world are independent of one another is of major importance in the *Tractatus*. For example,

The world divides into facts. [T 1.2]

Each can be the case or not the case, while the others remain the same. [T 1.21]

Later, when a fact has been analysed as the existence of elementary facts, Wittgenstein says:

Elementary facts are independent of one another. [T 2.061]

From the existence or non-existence of one elementary fact it is impossible to infer the existence or non-existence of another. [T 2.062]

The only type of dependence and independence which Wittgenstein recognises is the logical variety—'The only necessity is *logical* necessity' (T 6.37)—and accordingly what he means to dismiss is logical dependence between facts in the world. The purpose of the present chapter is to show that, although it is not stated in the text of the *Tractatus*, the Logical Independence Thesis is a consequence of the *Grundgedanke* (see Peterson, 1986b).

What the *Grundgedanke* does is to banish logical objects from the world: facts do not contain logical objects, and the logical constants do not function denotatively—they are not names, representatives, or proxies of objects in the factual world.

Discussing the Pictorial View that logical constants are names of logical objects, R.J. Fogelin says:

> From this it is an easy extension to think of logical truths as pictures of logical facts ... If there are logical facts, then the propositions expressing them will mutually imply each other and will be implied by every proposition whatsoever. Thus the doctrine of independence is lost. [*Wittgenstein*, p36]

and Fogelin concludes that the Pictorial View of the constants therefore

> ... presents a fundamental challenge to Wittgenstein's working out of a picture theory of proposition meaning within the framework of an atomistic ontology. [*loc cit*]

This argument, which appeals to one of the paradoxes of classical entailment (tautological implication), shows that on the Pictorial View of the constants, 'logical facts' will exist in the world, and, since each of these will be entailed by every fact, the Logical Independence Thesis will be lost. For example, on the Pictorial View 'Either it's raining or it's not raining' depicts a logically necessary or tautological fact, and this is entailed by every fact, including itself. This argument does allow, though, that molecular but logically contingent facts might be logically independent of one another. Fogelin is right that this incompatibility exists between the Pictorial View and the Logical Independence Thesis, but, as will now be argued, the *Grundgedanke* plays a more basic rôle than he suggests: in denying the Pictorial View it does not just make room for the Independence Thesis, but rather it gives the reason for it.

The dyadic logical relations—entailment, equivalence, subcontrariety, inconsistency etc.—concern logical form rather than content. In the case of atomic sentences—those which contain no logical constants—we can say that $A = A$ and that $A \models A$; but apart from these trivial cases, logical relations require constants—they require that at least one of their terms have molecular form. And likewise in the case of the monadic logical properties of tautologousness and contradictoriness, logical constants are a prerequisite: there is no such thing as an atomic formal tautology or contradiction. If there were molecular facts—configurations of atomic facts and logical objects—then these too would have molecular logical form, and would bear logical relations to one another, and to atomic facts. But since the *Grundgedanke* and its supporting arguments establish that there are no logical objects in the world, which is to say that all facts are logically atomic, it follows that such logical properties and relations do not attach to facts in the world. Since the formal logical properties and relations require molecularity, these are excluded from the world of facts. Thus there are no relations of entailment, inconsistency etc. between facts: all facts are logically independent (and no facts are tautological or contradictory). The only logical relations of which facts could conceivably be terms are reflexive equivalence and entailment, but since these are relations between a fact and itself, they do not constitute counter-examples to the Logical Independence Thesis. The denial that there are logical objects *within* facts leads to the denial that there are logical relations *between* facts: the *Grundgedanke* therefore leads to the Logical Independence Thesis, and need not be seen as a merely defensive manoeuvre designed to render independence compatible with the picture theory.

The *Grundgedanke* denies the existence of molecular facts, and so what remains are (*1*) atomic sentences, (*2*) molecular sentences, and (*3*) atomic facts. Since logical relations and properties require molecularity, they are excluded from the world of facts. Given any two different facts, there can be no logical entailment, equivalence, contradiction etc. between them, and given any one fact, this cannot be tautologous or contradictory. The world is therefore logically vacuous: it contains no logical constants, and consequently it contains no formal logical properties or relations. What the *Grundgedanke* does for the 'material' logical constants, the consequent Logical Independence Thesis does for the 'strict' logical properties and relations. The logical constants are not names of entities which are constituents of facts, and signs for the logical properties and relations are not names for properties and relations which attach to facts. The logical independence of facts, then, is not a matter of stipulation or definition in the *Tractatus*, but is crucially a consequence of the *Grundgedanke*.

It is worth noting that in the arguments supporting the *Grundgedanke*, and in the connection with the Logical Independence Thesis, there is no point of dependence on the details of the Tractarian

ontology. The arguments presented have nothing to do with the idea
that facts consist ultimately of configurations of elementary objects,
and that these are depicted by structurally isomorphic elementary
sentences. What Wittgenstein's arguments establish, therefore, is
the logical vacuity of the factual world *tout court*, not just the logical
vacuity of the world as seen through the Tractarian ontology.

One point does arise, however, which applies specially to Tractarian elementary sentences. These are stated to be logically independent:

> It is a sign of a sentence's being elementary that there can be no
> elementary sentence contradicting it. [T 4.211]

> One elementary sentence cannot be deduced from another. [T 5.134;
> cf T 5.152]

The point is a consequence of the *Grundgedanke* and the multiplicity requirement, and it applies generally to all logical properties
and relations, not just to to contradiction and entailment. First, an
elementary sentence consists only of names, and logical constants
are not names, therefore the elementary sentence will be logically
atomic, and therefore devoid of logical properties or relations (except of course the property of logical contingency). Second, an elementary fact will not, according to the *Grundgedanke*, contain any
logical objects. And by the picture theory's multiplicity requirement,
elementary sentences must not contain spare components. Thus an
elementary sentence—a sentence which is of the right sort to depict an elementary fact—will contain no logical constants. Since
elementary sentences are logically atomic, and since formal logical
properties and relations require molecularity, it follows again that
elementary sentences are logically contingent and that they are logically independent of one another.

The *Grundgedanke* does not however exclude all quasi-logical relations between facts, and as Wittgenstein later saw, considerations
of colour—or for that matter of other determinables—are problematic (see, for example, Wittgenstein's 'Remarks on Logical Form').
Nevertheless, it is by no means clear that there can be incompati-
bilities between colour-facts in the world. Since red and green are
incompatible, for example, it cannot simultaneously be the case both
that X is uniformly red and that X is uniformly green. That is, it

cannot be that the world contains at one time a fact corresponding to each of these two descriptions. But since these facts cannot simultaneously exist, they cannot bear a relation to one another, whether this is a relation of incompatibility or any other: the instantiation of a relation requires relata. Just as I cannot disagree with a non-existent person, so a colour-fact cannot be incompatible with a non-existent colour-fact. Thus, whatever analysis is to be given of colour incompatibility, it cannot involve incompatibility between *facts* in the world, whether these are taken to be Tractarian *Sachverhalte* or not.

Finally, what the *Grundgedanke* actually establishes is the absence from the world of the relations and properties studied in Formal Logic: it is not established that facts are independent *tout court*. To turn the Logical Independence Thesis into a general independence thesis, it has to be added that there is no necessity other than logical necessity, as is asserted without supporting argument in the 6.3's.

Chapter 6

The Nature of Logic

Introduction

The Tractarian view of the nature of logic is that logical properties and relations are structural and syntactic, and are internal to sentences themselves: so long as the rules governing the constants are given, these properties and relations hold independently of factors external to the sentences to which they attach. As he put it in 1914, during the early development of the Tractarian system:

> Logic takes care of itself; all we have to do is look and see how it does it. [N, p11; cf N, p1; N, p43; T 5.473]

and as Friedrich Waismann and Desmond Lee record, he said some years after the publication of the *Tractatus*, in 1930 and 1931:

> That inference is *a priori* means only that syntax decides whether an inference is right or wrong. [WN, p92]
>
> The $\therefore$ which we write in $p \therefore p \lor q$ is a sign of the same kind as $=$; it is about symbols. [LN, p58]

Being syntactic, logic is independent of facts; and being internal, logical properties and relations are independent of such external factors as the derivability of theorems from primitive, self-evident axioms.

The presentation of this case in the *Tractatus* is, unfortunately, obscured by two principal factors. First, the arguments given are only partially co-ordinated: they are presented in a piecemeal fashion, and it is not always made clear how they fit together. And second, the views Wittgenstein attacks are not given much explicit description: he does not proceed in the usual way by identifying his target, together with its sub-theses and possible variations, and then criticising it. As is often the case in the *Tractatus*, something of general importance becomes a background for detailed discussion of more particular points.

Wittgenstein's arguments can be grouped under three headings.

1. The negative Logical Independence Thesis, deriving from the *Grundgedanke*, banishes logical properties and relations from the world of facts: there are no logically necessary facts, and no logical relations of entailment, inconsistency etc. between facts.

2. The truth-conditional analysis of logical properties and relations, discussed below, shows that these can be explained by appeal only to the syntactic structures of sentences—and not to facts.

3. The discussion of the internal and structural nature of logical properties and relations shows again that these inhere in sentences themselves—and not in facts.

Wittgenstein's two main targets are what might be called (*1*) the 'Scientific View' of logic, and (*2*) the 'Axiomatic View'. The Scientific View, which Wittgenstein had encountered in Russell, is the thesis that logic belongs to the world: that there are logical facts whose existence is logically necessary, and that Logic is a fact-stating, representational science. According to this view a 'sentence of logic' would depict a logically necessary fact. The Axiomatic View consists of a cluster of philosophical assumptions which one might attach to the formal methods of axiomatic logic: primarily the proposals that axioms are self-evident and primitive, and that theorems are dependent on or 'justified' by them. What these two views have in common is an *external* interpretation of logic: on the Scientific View, the necessary truth of 'sentences of logic' is 'taken care of' by the corresponding logical facts, and on the Axiomatic View it is taken care of by self-evident axioms.

In opposition to these external views, Wittgenstein advances an *internal* account, to the effect that logical properties and relations are there in sentences themselves, and are not taken care of by external factors such as facts or axioms. On this view, statements about logical properties and relations are non-representational: they lack 'sense', they do not concern the world, they 'say nothing' (T 6.11), and they do not constitute a 'body of doctrine' (T 6.13) or a 'science'. As early as 1912 Wittgenstein had written to Russell:

> Logic must turn out to be of a TOTALLY different kind than any other science. [LR, p10]

For Wittgenstein it is natural science alone which studies the empirical world, and logic is not part of its subject matter—not even a part consisting of facts of a very general nature. Thus:

> Our fundamental principle is that whenever a question can be decided by logic at all it must be possible to decide it without more ado.
>
> (And if we get into a position where we have to look at the world for an answer to such a problem, that shows that we are on completely the wrong track.) [T 5.551]

In the *Tractatus* this is given detailed discussion, and the point that logic is syntactic rather than factual is approached from various angles. The special character of logic is to be explained not by its involving facts of a special logically necessary or self-evident sort, but by its not concerning facts at all.

The Truth-Conditional Analysis of Logical Properties and Relations

As mentioned above, the theory of truth-functions plays two very different rôles within the framework of the *Tractatus*. On one hand it gives a positive treatment of the logical connectives, and so, together with the conjunction/disjunction theory of quantification, it completes the Tractarian account of representational language. On the other hand, it plays a vital rôle in advancing Wittgenstein's thesis of the syntactic nature of logic, and the non-representational character of statements about logic. It plays this latter rôle by providing an exact technical analysis of logical properties and relations which depends only on the structures of sentences themselves, and which involves no reference to the world of facts. Logical properties and relations are analysed in terms of the truth-conditions of sentences, and these are determined, not by anything in the world, but by the logical structures of the sentences involved.

Of the logical properties of tautologousness and logical falsehood ('contradiction') Wittgenstein says:

> Among the possible groups of truth-conditions there are two extreme cases.
>
> In one of these cases the sentence is true for all the truth-possibilities of the elementary sentences. We say that the truth-conditions are *tautological*.
>
> In the second case the sentence is false for all the truth-possibilities: the truth-conditions are *contradictory*.
>
> In the first case we call the sentence a tautology; in the second, a contradiction. [T 4.46]

As already stated, it is not essential to the theory of truth-functions that the component sentences be elementary in the Tractarian sense, but Wittgenstein's meaning is clear. A tautology is such that every one of the relevant truth-possibilities is a truth-ground of the sentence; and a 'contradiction' is such that every one of the relevant truth-possibilities is a falsity-ground of the sentence.

At any time, precisely one of the relevant truth-possibilities must actually obtain—they form a determinable or 'space'. A tautology says nothing because it excludes none of them, and so it does nothing to narrow down the possibilities; and a contradiction says nothing because it excludes them all, and so contributes nothing to selecting the right one. Tautology and contradiction are therefore 'degenerate' cases of representational sentences: they are of the general type of representational sentences, but due to their truth-conditions, they actually say nothing.

The point for the philosophy of logic is that the 'logical truth' of a *Satz der Logic* is due to its *syntactic form*, for it is this which determines the statement's truth-conditions, and these in turn determine that it is a tautology.

Axiomatic logical systems may help *us* to discover which statements are logical truths, and they may give some statements the status of axioms, but this is *logically* beside the point. The logical truth of the statement resides *in the statement itself*, and whatever axiomatic systems may do, one tautology is as good as another. And further, a logically true statement may be universally true, but this does not mean, as Russell had thought, that it states a fact of a universal character. Rather, it is a tautology because of its syntactic form, and so *any* statement of that form will be a tautology. The element of universality is thus intra-linguistic, and has nothing to do with the world.

In making his case, Wittgenstein concentrates on the monadic logical property of tautologousness, simply because of the central rôle which tautologies played in the axiomatic logic of the day. But the case naturally extends to the dyadic, and other, logical relations: entailment, inconsistency, sub-contrariety, and so on.

Wittgenstein takes the relation of entailment or logical consequence to be that of strict or 'tautological' implication, and this he defines by saying:

> In particular the truth of a sentence 'p' follows from the truth of another sentence 'q' if all the truth-grounds of the latter are truth-grounds of the former. [T 5.12]

That is, the truth-grounds of the antecedent contain those of the consequent. This again is a purely syntactic matter: it concerns only truth-conditions, and these are wholly determined by the arrangement of logical constants in the sentence—and it is for this reason that they can be calculated using the truth-table method. Each logical connective has an associated set of truth-conditions, as indicated in its truth-table, and in a complex sentence, these all resolve together to determine a set of truth-conditions for the sentence as a whole. Truth-conditions are determined by the syntactic structures of the sentences, and not by anything in the factual world, and accordingly the relation of logical consequence can be disovered by using formal proof techniques whose only input is the sentences themselves. So logical relations *between* sentences, just like logical properties of single sentences, concern syntax alone.[1]

---

[1]In the context of the sentential calculus, the other logical relations can also

This analysis extends to the predicate calculus, given the conjunction/disjunction account of quantification discussed in chapter 4. The *Tractatus* provides just what is needed at this point: an account of logical properties and relations which appeals to nothing extra-linguistic, and allows their reality to inhere inside the mirror of representational language.

Internality

Wittgenstein frequently expressed his view that logic is syntactic by saying that logical properties and relations are '*internal*' to sentences themselves. (Cf. the use of 'internal' in Bradley, 1897; and Moore 1922, chapter IX.) If sentences are given, then their truth-conditions are thereby also given, and since logical properties and relations are a matter of the truth-conditions of sentences, these are given too. The truth-conditional analysis of strict-implication appears in the 5.1's and 5.2's, and this is closely followed by some key remarks on the internality of this logical relation.

> When the truth of one sentence follows from the truth of others, we can see this from the structure of the sentences. [T 5.13]

> If the truth of one sentence follows from the truth of others, this finds expression in the relations in which the forms of the sentences stand to one another: nor is it necessary for us to set up these relations between them, by combining them with one another in a single sentence; on the contrary, the relations are internal, and their existence is an immediate result of the existence of the sentences themselves. [T 5.131]

> The structures of sentences stand in internal relations to one another. [T 5.2; cf N, p32]

---

be given a purely truth-functional analysis, here given in terms of falsity grounds. Given sentences S and T, and the set P of truth-possibilities generated by the set of the components of S and T: S and T are inconsistent iff their falsity grounds are jointly exhaustive of P, S and T are subcontraries iff there is no falsity ground common to them both, S and T are proper contradictories iff they are both inconsistent and subcontrary, and S and T are logically equivalent iff they have the same falsity grounds.

The phrase 'combining them with one another in a single sentence' refers to the procedure used in axiomatic deduction whereby sentences are combined, for example into a material implication sentence, and this is then demonstrated to be a tautology (see below). However this is not constitutive of the logical relation: the 'structures'—the logical forms—of the sentences determine their truth-conditions, and it is these in turn which determine the logical relation.

On the relation of contradiction, Wittgenstein says in the *Notebooks*:

> How does the *sentence* '∼p' really contradict the *sentence* '*p*'? The internal relations of the two signs must mean contradiction. [N, p32]

And there is a corresponding remark in the *Tractatus*:

> If two sentences contradict one another, then their structure shows it; and the same is true if one of them follows from another. And so on. [T 4.211]

When we investigate the logical relations between sentences, we are investigating what is already there in those sentences. We do not create anything, and the logical relations do not depend on our proofs for their existence:

> We have said that some things are arbitrary in the symbols that we use and that some things are not. In logic it is only the latter that express: but that means that logic is not a field in which *we* express what we wish with the help of signs, but rather one in which the nature of the natural and inevitable signs speaks for itself. If we know the logical syntax of any sign-language, then we have already been given the sentences of logic. [T 6.124]

Compare:

> *The sentence itself* must show that it says *something* and in the case of the tautology that it says nothing. [N, p55]

If logical properties and relations depended on something outside the sentences they connected—if they were not internal to those sentences—then they would not be autonomous: they would be taken care of by the world, by self-evidence etc. But since logical relations hold in virtue of the forms of the sentences involved, logic is autonomous—it does not need any outside help, and 'takes care of itself'. To be precise: it is sentences which take care of the logical relations among them—they are objective and independent of external assistance. *We* take care of proofs, and what we are proving, or rather discovering, takes care of itself, just as *we* take care of a telescope, while the planet we discover by means of it takes care of itself: the proof procedures of Formal Logic are methods of discovery rather than methods of creation.

Thus, logical properties and relations attach to *sentences* in virtue of their internal, syntactic structures, and are not determined by such external considerations as the state of the world, self-evidence, or deducibility from axioms—logic takes care of itself.

The topic of internality also arises, as mentioned above, in Wittgenstein's discussion of the picture theory of meaning. Here Wittgenstein asserts that the relation of depiction between elementary sentence and elementary fact is internal, so that the elementary sentence depicts 'as it were off its own bat' (N, p26). The internality thesis regarding depiction and that regarding logical relations have the common factor that each suggests that, in different senses, language 'takes care of itself'. But the two theses are distinct, since the first concerns relations between sentence and fact—the 'vertical' type—while the second concerns relations between sentence and sentence—the 'horizontal' type. In the *Tractatus*, these two internality theses are largely, and rightly, kept apart, but there are some indications (for example at T 4.125) that Wittgenstein was tempted to conflate them.

The Axiomatic Method

Before further examining Wittgenstein's views on the nature of logic, it is worth considering the axiomatic method of logical proof which prevailed at the time Wittgenstein wrote the *Tractatus*, and which provides a context and a target for many of his remarks.

The logical system of *Principia Mathematica*, which Wittgenstein encountered early on, is of a Euclidean, axiomatic character. Certain logical truths are treated as primitive axioms, and rules of inference are then used to derive other logical truths as theorems from this axiomatic base. A typically Euclidean device is used which allows abbreviation of proofs, which tend to be long and complex: once a theorem has been demonstrated, it is numbered and used in later proofs. As a result, the proofs are not independent, but form an interrelated system. An example of a proof from the *Principia* is:[2]

*2.12. $\vdash .p \supset \sim(\sim p)$
  Dem.
  2.11 $\dfrac{\sim p}{p}$ $\vdash . \sim p \vee \sim(\sim p)$ (1)

  $[(1).(*1.01)]$ $\vdash .p \supset \sim(\sim p)$

[*Principia Mathematica*, p101].

The first line of the proof says that the previously demonstrated theorem *2.11 (which is '$p \vee \sim p$'), when '$\sim p$' is substituted for 'p', yields the sentence '$\sim p \vee \sim(\sim p)$', which within the proof is numbered as (1). The second line says that by applying the Definition *1.01, which is '$p \supset q. = . \sim p \vee q$', to (1) we derive '$p \supset \sim(\sim p)$'. In this way a new theorem is derived, and given the soundness of the system, and the correctness of the proof, this will be a logical truth.

Such a system can of course be interpreted as a 'black box'— simply as a mechanism whose output consists of logical truths—and there is no compulsion to attach particular philosophical significance to the details of its operation. However, since the system works with logically true sentences, rather than with premises and conclusions, the impression is naturally given that the property of logical truth is somehow more essential to logic than are the logical relations. And further, it is not unnatural to suppose that the axioms of the system are *self-evident* and *logically primitive* and serve to *justify* the derived theorems. The first of these assumptions had some influence on the way in which Wittgenstein presented his case, with the result that many of his remarks on logic are couched in terms of the monadic property of logical truth, rather than in terms of the various logical

---

[2]In the dialect of the sentential calculus used here, the dot sign is used to indicate scope.

relations which obtain *between* sentences; but he was highly critical of the other suppositions mentioned.

The output of an axiomatic system consists—if the system is sound and the proofs are properly constructed—of logically true sentences written in the object language, such as '$p \supset \sim(\sim p)$' in the example above. Wittgenstein called such sentences *Sätze der Logic* or *logische Sätze*, which will be translated here as 'sentences of logic' (and which Ogden, and Pears and McGuinness, translate as 'propositions of logic'). The German *Satz* means 'sentence' or 'proposition', and is also used to mean 'theorem' or 'principle'. *Sätze der Logic* are simply logically true sentences, as appear both as the axioms and the theorems of an axiomatic system, and Wittgenstein's analysis of these is that they are tautologies. Special importance is attached in the use of such a system to theorems which are material implication sentences, since these allow us to demonstrate the validity of arguments—to show that their premises entail their conclusions. The procedure by which this is done is as follows. Given an argument, a material implication sentence is formed which takes the conjunction of the premises of the argument as its antecedent, and the conclusion of the argument as its consequent. By constructing a proof in the axiomatic system, we show that this sentence is a theorem of the system, and therefore that it is a tautology, and therefore that the original argument is valid. For example, to validate the argument:

$$p \supset q$$
$$\underline{\quad p \quad}$$
$$\therefore \quad q$$

we form the sentence '$((p \supset q) \;\&\; p) \supset q$', and derive it as a theorem in the system. This manoeuvre relies on the principle that $\models A \supset B$ iff $A \models B$: that is, a sentence whose main connective is the material implication sign is logically true iff its antecedent entails its consequent.[3] As Wittgenstein puts it:

> That the sentences '$p \supset q$', 'p', and 'q', combined with one another in the form '$(p \supset q).(p) : \supset : (q)$', yield a tautology shows that q follows from p and $p \supset q$. [T 6.1201; cf WN, p219; MN1, p117]

---

[3]The expression 'iff' is shorthand for 'if and only if'.

For example if your tautology is of the form $p \supset q$ you can see that q follows from p; and so on. [MN1, p112]

The logically true sentence thus gives the form of an argument (see 6.1264), since if we substitute 'therefore' for the material implication sign we get a (rather short) *valid* argument. Axiomatic logic, then, gives a specially central rôle to logically true *Sätze der Logic*, and this together with the cluster of assumptions concerning self-evidence, primitiveness, and justification will be discussed in the sections below.

Tautologies

Wittgenstein's positive account of the nature of logical properties and relations is adequately presented in the remarks so far discussed, in which he argues that they are internal and syntactic in character. However, under the influence of axiomatic logic, and its manoeuvre of deriving statements of logical relations from statements of logically true sentences, Wittgenstein also presents his view in terms of the latter. For instance, since '$\models A \supset B$' is true iff '$A \models B$' holds, philosophical points made about the first can be transferred to the second. In particular, since tautologousness is syntactic, and tautologies say nothing about the world, the same goes for logic and statements about logic in general. Thus:

> It is the peculiar mark of sentences of logic that one can recognise that they are true from the symbol alone, and this fact contains in itself the whole philosophy of logic. And so too it is a very important fact that the truth or falsity of sentences which do not belong to logic *cannot* be recognised from the sentence alone.[4][T 6.113]

An odd stylistic point is that, although Wittgenstein makes it clear within certain remarks that they are principles of his philosophy of logic, the Tractarian numbering system does not indicate this. At 4.0312 we have the *Grundgedanke* or 'fundamental thought', 5.551 gives his 'fundamental principle', and the 'whole philosophy of logic' is given at T 6.113. In any case, T 6.113 is comparable with:

---

[4]The word *schließt*, here translated as 'contains' also carries the connotation of secure fastening.

It is impossible to tell from the picture alone whether it is true or false. [T 2.224]

And a very similar statement of the view appears as early as 1913 in a letter written to Russell from Norway (LR, p39). Wittgenstein speaks in terms of how *we* recognise that a sentence is logically true, but the essential point is that the property of logical truth of such a sentence is present in the sentential sign itself, and not in anything outside it (and hence in order to discover it we must examine the sentence itself, and not the world).

Although what is said in the *Tractatus* about tautologies transfers automatically to the other logical properties and relations, the concentration on one logical property is rather artificial. In the first place, the examples he gives of tautologies are almost all of those which have the material implication sign as their main connective (see T 6.1264). But a tautology of the sentential calculus may have any of the other connectives as its main connective, and in these cases the logical relation which is most directly inferred from the tautologousness of the sentence is not that of entailment. For example, $\models A \mid B$ iff A is inconsistent with B (where '|' indicates alternative denial), $\models A \equiv B$ iff A is logically equivalent to B etc. For any connective $\otimes$ we can infer, from the tautologousness of a sentence whose main connective is $\otimes$, that one of the logical relations obtains between the two main components of the sentence:

$\models A \supset B$ iff A entails B

$\models A \mid B$ iff A is inconsistent with B

$\models A \vee B$ iff A and B are subcontraries

$\models A \equiv B$ iff A and B are logically equivalent

$\models A + B$ iff A and B are proper contradictories

Thus tautologies using any of the dyadic connectives can be made to play the rôle Wittgenstein gives in his discussion to those which are materially implicative: in each case we can infer, from a sentence's having the monadic logical property of tautologousness, that a dyadic logical relation holds between its two main components. It must be said, though, that in Wittgenstein's formal definition of tautologousness there is no restriction on what is the main connective of a tautology.

And further, as Wittgenstein mentions at one point in the *Tractatus*, in this procedure of deriving a dyadic logical relation from a monadic logical property, we can use 'contradictions' (inconsistencies) instead of tautologies. After saying that the tautologousness of a material implication sentence shows that its antecedent entails its consequent (T 6.1201), Wittgenstein writes:

> It is clear that one could achieve the same purpose by using contradictions instead of tautologies. [T 6.1202]

The correlations are not quite so straightforward, but using the sign '||' to indicate inconsistency we have, for example:

$||$ $\sim(A \supset B)$ iff A entails B

$||$ $\sim(A \mid B)$ iff A and B are inconsistent

$||$ $\sim(A \vee B)$ iff A and B are subcontraries

$||$ $\sim(A \equiv B)$ iff A and B are logically equivalent

$||$ $\sim(A + B)$ iff A and B are proper contradictories

Indeed, some logical systems are in practice used in this way: the inconsistency of a sentence of one of these forms is proved in the system, and the holding of the corresponding logical relation is inferred. As Wittgenstein says (T 4.462), contradictions, like tautologies, are non-representational and tell us nothing about the world. I learn nothing about the world if I am told 'Either it is raining or it isn't', and equally I learn nothing if I am told 'It is raining and it isn't'. Thus, the philosophy of logic could just as well be focused on contradictions as on tautologies.

The procedure whereby we start with a statement of one of the monadic logical properties of tautologousness and contradiction, and derive a statement of a dyadic logical relation, might be called the 'monadic method'. However there is really nothing logically essential about this, and its feasibility is just one result of the inter-derivability of logical properties and relations. Later, in 1930, Wittgenstein made it clear in a conversation recorded by Waismann that he recognised that the monadic method is not essential and that 'Tautologies are only one way of showing what is syntactic' (WN, p92).

Thus, we do not have to approach logic in the monadic manner; and if we do, we do not have to concentrate on tautologies; and if we do this, we do not have to restrict ourselves to those whose main connective is material implication. These restrictions in Wittgenstein's exposition in the 6.1's do not themselves create serious difficulties for his thesis that logic is syntactic, but merely manifest the influence on his thought of the axiomatic method, in which the theorems are tautologies, and in practice usually have material implication as their main connective. In this context, the Naïve Representationalist view of logic crystallises in the thought that logically true statements express logically necessary facts, and so it is that Wittgenstein takes such trouble to replace this with his syntactic account.

Related Issues

Saying Nothing

It is worth noting that the saying-nothing of tautologies (T 6.11) does not in itself support the Tractarian view of the nature of logic. The tautologous *Sätze der Logic*, especially in the rôle they play in axiomatic logic, might seem to be principles of logic, and since they 'say' nothing in Wittgenstein's technical sense, we might seem on this basis to be led to the desired conclusion that logic is non-factual. There are two main reasons why this is not the case.

First, tautologous sentences are not themselves principles of logic: they are not statements about logic at all. It is true that what is written on the bottom line of a proof in an axiomatic system is such a sentence, but it is not the case that what the proof demonstrates is simply the truth of this sentence. In the example from *Principia Mathematica* above '$p \supset \sim(\sim p)$' is written on the bottom line of the proof, but it is not the case that the import of the proof is the demonstration that $p \supset \sim(\sim p)$. Rather, the proof demonstrates that '$p \supset \sim(\sim p)$' *is a tautology*: it proves that $\models p \supset \sim(\sim p)$. And regarding '$p \models \sim(\sim p)$', this is inferred from '$\models p \supset \sim(\sim p)$', and cannot be inferred from '$p \supset \sim(\sim p)$'. The sentence at the bottom of an axiomatic proof does not appear in isolation but at the bottom of the proof, and the point of the proof is that—assuming the soundness of the system and the correctness of the proof—it has been demonstrated to be a tautology. Thus, although in axiomatic logic a central rôle is played by tautologies, it is the tautologousness of these sentences, rather than their truth, which is essential. And the main principle which allows them to play this rôle is that $\models A \supset B$ iff $A \models B$, which is not at all the same as $A \supset B$ iff $A \models B$.

Statements about logic are *metalinguistic*: even if we restrict ourselves to tautologies we do not just state the tautologous sentence— we state *that it is a tautology*. Simply writing '$p \supset \sim(\sim p)$' conveys nothing about logic: to state that the sentence is tautologous we must write '$\models p \supset \sim(\sim p)$'. If I learn that 'Either it's raining or it isn't' is true then I learn nothing about the world of facts, and I also learn nothing about logic; but if I learn that the sentence is tautologous, then I do learn something about logic. A logic book which contained nothing but a mixture of tautologies and logical contingencies would not convey much about logic, but one which stated which were which could convey a great deal, and could give a basis for valid inferences. The peculiar mark of *Sätze der Logic* is not just that we can recognise from the symbol alone that they are true (T 6.113), but that we can recognise from the symbol alone that they are tautologous.

Second, the saying-nothing of a tautology is of the wrong sort, since it is too broad. In Wittgenstein's technical sense, a statement 'says nothing' if it is not fact-stating—if it says nothing about the world. But the vacuity of a tautology is more extreme than this: a tautology is wholly uninformative, and tells us nothing about the world, logic, or anything else; and so tautologies 'say nothing' in the ordinary, non-technical sense. The potential confusion is between two senses of 'say': in Wittgenstein's technical sense, statements about logic 'say' nothing about the world of facts, and in a general and non-technical sense, tautologies 'say' nothing at all, and the two are not equivalent.

By analogy, if we wanted to show that certain psychological statements were about the non-physical mind rather than the brain, we might support this case by showing that these statements said nothing about the brain. But if what we really showed were that these statements were wholly uninformative, and said nothing at all, then the argument would not support the conclusion.

Universal Truth

In making out the case that logic is syntactic, Wittgenstein opposed himself to Russell, who entertained the view that Logic is a science

whose concern is to state logical facts. For example, in 1919 Russell
wrote:

> Logic is concerned with the real world just as truly as zoology,
> though with its more abstract and general features. [*Introduction
> to Mathematical Philosophy*, p169]

It is of course evident that if the discipline of Logic is a science
whose subject matter is the world, it is nevertheless somewhat different from other sciences. The differentia most naturally appealed to
is that of universal or general truth, and on this view the peculiarity
of logic is that it is concerned with the most abstract and general of
truths. Accordingly Russell wrote in 1913:

> Every logical notion, in a very important sense, is or involves a
> *summum genus*, and results from a process of generalisation which
> has been carried to its utmost limit. This is a peculiarity of logic,
> and a touchstone by which logical propositions may be distin-
> guished from all others. ['Theory of Knowledge', p97; cf *Principles
> of Mathematics*, p xii]

Thus, for example, '$(p \mathbin{\&} q) \supset q$' is a truth of logic, and on this
view its being so consists in the universality of its truth—in its being
true of all sentences p and q. As in algebra, the sentence's variables
are bound by implicit universal quantifiers, so it might be written
as '$(p)(q)((p \mathbin{\&} q) \supset q)$': the sentence says that for *all* sentences p
and q it is true that '$(p \mathbin{\&} q) \supset q$' (cf LR, p10). Wittgenstein did not
deny that such sentences are universally true, but held that this is
not their essential characteristic:

> The mark of a sentence of logic is *not* general validity. To be
> general means no more than to be accidentally valid for all things.
> An ungeneralised sentence can be tautological just as well as a
> generalised one. [T 6.1231]

For Wittgenstein the touchstone of logical truth is tautologousness, and universality is not essential. Thus the sentence 'Either it
is raining or it is not raining' is tautologous, and hence is a logical
truth, although it is not a general truth, since it contains several
constants other than its two logical constants 'or' and 'not'. On the

other hand, if a sentence expresses a universal truth, this alone is not enough to make it a logical truth. It is not the generality of Logic (manifested in its use of variables) which differentiates it from natural science, but rather its subject matter, which is syntactic rather than factual. Russell, however, persisted in his view, and in 1937 he wrote:

> In the first place, no proposition of logic can mention any particular object. The statement 'If Socrates is a man and all men are mortal, then Socrates is mortal' is not a proposition of logic. [*Principles of Mathematics*, 2nd ed., p xi]

On the Tractarian view, however, a logically true statement need not be *explicitly* universal, but universality is built into it: its logical truth derives from its tautologous logical form, and as a consequence *any* statement with the same form will be logically true.

Self-Evidence

As well as attacking the Scientific View of logic, Wittgenstein aims some of his remarks at the Axiomatic View that the axioms in an axiomatic system are in no need of proof since their truth is self-evident, that they have a special primitive status, and that the theorems of the system are somehow dependent upon or justified by their derivation from the axioms. As already mentioned, we are under no compulsion to adopt this interpretation of axiomatic deduction, and such systems can be viewed as 'black boxes', without attaching philosophical significance to the details of their operation. The effect of Wittgenstein's remarks, therefore, is not to discredit axiomatic deduction itself, but is to discredit a cluster of interpretive assumptions.

Regarding self-evidence, Wittgenstein says:

> ...it is remarkable that a thinker so exact as Frege should have appealed to the degree of self-evidence as the criterion of a logical sentence. [T 6.1271]

> If the truth of a sentence does not *follow* from its being self-evident to us, then its self evidence in no way justifies our belief in its truth. [T 5.1363]

The 'self evidence' of which Russell has talked so much can only be dispensed with in logic if language itself prevents any logical mistake. And it is clear that that 'self-evidence' is and always was wholly deceptive. [N, p4; cf N, p3; T 5.4731]

For Wittgenstein, logical truth is to be found in the sentences themselves, and not in anything so extraneous or as subjective as self-evidence. Wittgenstein's use of 'mistake', like his use of 'surprise' and 'discovery', is rather strange—the point is that logic itself cannot go wrong, not that *we* cannot be mistaken. Clearly a *person* might say that '$p \& q$' entails '$(p \lor q) \supset \sim p$', and would thus be mistaken; but logic would 'take care of itself' and the relation which does hold between these sentences—that of inconsistency—would still obtain. In a sense, though, if we discover a new tautology, for example, this is not a real discovery, since we were in possession in the first place of the rules governing the connectives, and it is these which make the sentence tautologous.

For universal truth and self-evidence Wittgenstein substitutes tautologousness as the criterion of logical truth. When studying logic we are therefore not concerned with the world or with an epistemological relation between ourselves and sentences, but with properties of sentences themselves.

Primitiveness

As well as denying self-evidence as the special mark of logical truths, Wittgenstein also denies any special primitive status to axioms:

> All the sentences of logic are of equal status: it is not the case that some of them are essentially primitive sentences and others essentially derived sentences. Every tautology itself shows that it is a tautology. [T 6.127]

> It is clear that the number of the 'primitive sentences of logic' is arbitrary, since one could derive logic from a single primitive sentence, for example, by simply constructing the logical product of Frege's primitive sentences. (Frege would perhaps say that we should then no longer have an immediately self-evident primitive sentence. But it is remarkable that a thinker as rigorous as Frege appealed to the degree of self-evidence as the criterion of a logical sentence.) [T 6.1271]

Thus, although in a particular axiomatic system the tautologies which play the rôle of axioms are primitive, this is simply a matter of the mechanics of the system in question: no special *logical* status is thereby conferred on these sentences. If we took the logical truth of sentences to consist in their being provable within a particular system, then the axioms of that system might seem to have a special logical status. But when tautologousness is substituted as the criterion of logical truth, this impression disappears. And since the axioms of a system are not logically primitive, there is a degree of arbitrariness in which logical truths we choose as axioms. This same puzzle, that on the one hand the primitive axioms of a system seem to act as its basis, while on the other hand their choice is somewhat arbitrary, arose also in ancient Greece *vis a vis* Euclidian geometry. It was recognised then also that there is some degree of choice in picking geometrical axioms, and therefore that the assertion that a particular set of axioms is *the* basis of geometry is dubious.

Justification

Wittgenstein takes 'justification' in a logical rather than an epistemological sense. His thought is that, given that logical relations take care of themselves, a proof in a logical system which demonstrates to us that a logical relation holds is just that—it is a method by which *we* discover that the relation holds, and does not justify, create, establish, or support the relation itself. Wittgenstein's view forbids the idea that the proof somehow gives the ground for the relation: the proof is quite external to the relation itself, and for that matter everything outside the sentences in question is external to the relation. The 'Notes on Logic' of 1913 contain clear statements of this idea.

> Deduction only proceeds according to the laws of deduction but these laws cannot justify the deduction. [NL, p93]

> Logical inferences can it is true, be made in accordance with Frege's or Russell's laws of deduction, but this cannot justify the inference; and therefore they are not primitive sentences of logic. If p follows from q, it can be inferred from q, and the 'manner of deduction' is indifferent. [NL, p100]

And in the *Tractatus* the view is further developed.

If p follows from q, I can make an inference from q to p, deduce p from q.

The nature of the inference can be gathered only from the two sentences.

They themselves are the only possible justification of the inference.

'Laws of inference', which are supposed to justify inferences, as in the works of Frege and Russell, have no sense, and would be superfluous. [T 5.132; cf 5.13, 5.1311]

The use of the subjunctive 'would' in the last sentence quoted is significant. Rules of inference may be superfluous to logic—to real logical relations—but in the absence of a new logical method to replace those which use rules of inference, they cannot be called superfluous to *us*. At present, we need them in order to prove theorems, and discover logical truths. When Wittgenstein says they 'would' be superfluous, he means that they would be so if a perspicuous logical notation based on his principles were devised (see chapter 7).

In the lectures which Wittgenstein gave in 1931, after his return to Cambridge, he made very similar statements, as recorded in Desmond Lee's notes:

Inference is the transition from one sentence to another, a transition which we justify by saying, for example, that q follows from p. This relation is entirely determined when the two sentences are given. It is entirely different from other relations, in which the opposite case is always thinkable. The relation of following and similar relations are internal relations and hold when (roughly) it is unthinkable that they should not hold. Whether a sentence is true or false can only be decided by comparison with reality. So that $p \lor q$ follows from $p \cdot q$ is not a sentence: it has no sense. What justifies the inference is seeing the internal relation. No rule of inference is needed to justify the inference, since if it were I would need another rule to justify the rule and that would lead to an infinite regress. We must see the internal relation. [LN, p56]

An internal relation holds by virtue of the terms being what they are. Inference is justified by an internal relation which we see; the only justification of the transition is our looking at the two terms and seeing the internal relation between them. [LN, p57]

There is some confusion here between the actual internality of a logical relation, and our being able to see that the relation holds— between the questions of internality and manifestness. It may be that if we really knew what we meant by the sentences involved, then we would also know that the relation obtains, but in cases of complex sentences the relation is not manifest. We cannot just *look* at

$$ `(p \vee (p \vee \sim q)) \ \& \ (q \vee (\sim r \supset p)) \ \& \ (\sim r \vee (p \vee q))` $$

and then at

$$ `p` $$

and simply '*see*' that they are logically equivalent. Indeed, if we used a different notation, it might be possible to do this, but in Russellian notation it cannot be done—we must calculate. As will be argued in the following chapter, Wittgenstein's principles do indicate that this *should* be possible, but that is not to say that in Russellian notation it *is* possible. It is one thing to say that the logical relation does not need our methods of proof to establish its existence, but it is another to say that we do not need them to discover it.

'World' and 'Logic'

The most natural reading of the earlier parts of the *Tractatus* is a realist one according to which the 'world' is the external, physical world, and 'facts' and 'elementary facts' are its constituents. However at some points later in the *Tractatus* (for example T 5.61), Wittgenstein uses the expression 'the world' to indicate something quite different—the world of phenomenal experience. Two options seem to be open. The first is to regard these as different uses of 'the world', and to interpret the *Tractatus* as an essentially realist work which uses a key term ambiguously. The second is to read Wittgenstein phenomenally, taking objects, elementary facts, and facts to be constituents of mental experience. This second reading (advocated by M.B. and J. Hintikka, 1985) has the advantage of consistency; but it has the disadvantage that Wittgenstein does not say that the objects, *Sachverhalte*, and *Tatsachen* which compose the world (T 1– 1.2) are phenomenal. What I have called the Tractarian 'ontology' is presented in a highly abstract way, and perhaps it is fairest to say that the book can be read in either way—which is not to say that it *is* an implicit doctrine of the *Tractatus* that objects, *Sachverhalte*, and *Tatsachen* are phenomenal.

In any case, the force of the arguments in the *Tractatus* concerning logic, probability, modality etc. is that these are syntactic and are not to be found in the world. (On a phenomenal reading, this would mean that they are not to be found in experience.) But we are left with a further problem, since Wittgenstein does use the word 'logic' in discussing the world. He speaks of the 'logical form' of objects and elementary facts (for example T 2.0233, 4.12) and of the 'logico-pictorial form' common to a picture and what it depicts (T 2.2). Here, though, what is involved is not the logic of argument, inference etc. as studied in Formal Logic, but rather the forms of combination of objects and names in elementary facts and elementary sentences, and these are issues of *factual form* and *pictorial form*, rather than logical form as normally understood. We are left with two conceptions of logic: first, there is the logic of the logical constants, which is the traditional subject of Formal Logic, and which according to the *Tractatus* is ultimately truth-functional; then, second, there is what might be called the 'pictorial/factual' logic of those 'logico-pictorial forms' common to sentences and the world they represent. It is indeed hard to see why the word 'logic' should be used in the second context, and its use seems to manifest confusion and wishful thinking. A set of sentences determines a set of truth-possibilities, and this is a determinable in the sense that at any one time exactly one of the set must be true. Analogously, a set of objects determines a set of possible-worlds, and this is again a determinable in the sense that at any one time exactly one will obtain. However, this similarity is hardly enough to justify Wittgenstein's broad use of 'logic', and it remains mysterious what sort of logic there is in a world devoid of logical properties and relations, in which all facts are logically atomic and logically independent.

Wittgenstein's broad use of 'logic' bears in particular on the interpretation of the second paragraph of the *Grundgedanke* in which he says '...there can be no representatives of the *logic* of facts' (T 4.0312). On one hand this phrase can be read as meaning that there can be no such thing as a logical constant which names a logical object resident in the factual world. And on the other hand, it can be read as meaning that the forms or configurations of elementary facts ('logical forms') cannot be represented in language (cf T 4.12). And both of these, of course, are doctrines of the *Tractatus*. At a number of points in the *Tractatus*, Wittgenstein makes statements which have more than one meaning, and this seems to be such a case (cf T 5.62, 6.4; and cf Ramsey's letter to his mother in LO, pp77–8).

What is clear is that Wittgenstein wanted to establish a connection between logic as usually understood, and the forms of elementary facts in the world ('pictorial/factual logic'), and he does sketch an argument to this effect. He says that logic is 'world mirroring' (T 5.511; cf T 6.13), and he appeals—as so often—to tautologies, saying that these show the 'logic of the world' (T 6.22), the 'scaffolding of the world' (T 6.124), and the 'formal—logical—properties of language and the world' (T 6.12) (see also Black, *Companion*). This line of thought is not wholly out of place in the *Tractatus*: it distinguishes between what a tautology says (nothing), and what it shows (the structure of the world); and it finds resonance with the remark where it is analogously claimed that scientific theory essentially concerns syntax, but is also connected with the world (T 6.342). However, the argument (given at T 6.124) is hardly convincing. The main premise is that tautologies 'presuppose that names have meaning and elementary sentences have sense' (T 6.124): since the names have sense, corresponding objects must exist, and since the elementary sentences have sense, the forms they have must be of the sort also to be found in elementary facts in the world. The idea seems to be that tautologies are inherently true in virtue of the internal feature of tautological form, and that they thus presuppose that their component sentences have sense, and so show something about the objects and forms to be found in world. However the notion of 'presupposition' involved here is suspect. Tautologousness actually involves two factors: first the component sentences should be well formed, and second the sentence as a whole should have tautological logical form. Now the first factor is not unique to tautologies, but is shared by contradictory and contingent sentences—indeed by any sentence which is well formed. What makes a well formed sentence tautologous is its logical form—the structure formed by its logical constants—and this has nothing further to do with its particular component sentences (which is why it is called a 'form').

Summary

In his journey inside the great mirror of language Wittgenstein gives more attention to logic than to any other topic. His conclusion is that logic is syntactic: there are no logical objects, and no logical facts, and any attempt to look for logic outside of sentences themselves is misguided.

Throughout the treatment of logic, the influence of the *Grundgedanke* can be felt: in the Logical Independence Thesis, in the appeal to the internal, structural nature of logical properties and relations, and in their truth-functional analysis, thus forming a complicated pattern of influence:

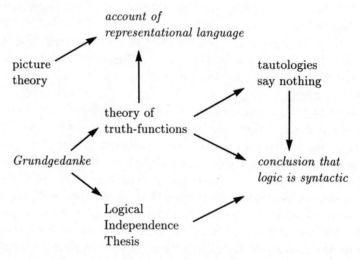

    In denying the pictorial account of the logical constants, the *Grundgedanke* leaves a gap which is filled by the theory of truth-functions. The theory of truth-functions, together with the picture theory of meaning, completes the Tractarian account of representational language, and it also serves the quite different purpose of providing a truth-conditional analysis of logical properties and relations, thus leading to the conclusion that logic belongs to the syntactic category. The *Grundgedanke* also leads to the Logical Independence Thesis, which complements the view that logic is syntactic, by asserting that logic does not belong to the world of facts. The *Grundgedanke* therefore bears on the rest of the *Tractatus* in a manner which is strong, but complex and by no means linear.

The Tractarian view of logic is consistently *internal*. Wittgenstein opposes Russell's external Scientific View that statements about logic are 'scientific' statements of worldly fact—albeit necessary or universal fact—whereby the statement would be dependent on the external fact for its truth. He also opposes the external Axiomatic View, which would make a logically true statement's character somehow dependent on the external apparatus of deduction from *other* primitive and self-evident statements. Accordingly he argues that the axioms in an axiomatic logical system are not *logically* primitive, that the criterion of their logical truth is not self-evidence, and that the deduction of a theorem from axioms is not what 'justifies' the logical truth of the theorem: the criterion of the logical truth of axioms and theorems alike is their syntactic structure—tautologous logical form.

Wittgenstein's perspective, as always, is the three-sided mirror, and his opponent is the Naïve Representationalist. His concern is not to make miscellaneous attacks on Frege or Russell, but to locate logic within his scheme. His answer is that it belongs to the syntactic category, and his various remarks—from the *Grundgedanke*, through the Logical Independence Thesis, the theory of truth-functions, and the remarks on internality, tautologies, universal truth, self-evidence, logical inference etc.—are all variations on this theme.

Details apart, what this amounts to is the assertion that logical properties and relations are to be found not in the world, but in language. The *Tractatus* therefore does for logical form what abstract art has done for geometrical form: instead of being treated as something in the world to be depicted, it is treated as a part of the representational system itself (see epilogue II). It has a life of its own, *inside* the mechanism of reflection, and 'takes care of itself'. It is independent of the world and nature, saying nothing about them, being neither confirmed nor refuted by them, and it is properly investigated as such. Nevertheless, its normal rôle is as part of the great representational mirror, and in this way it is connected to the world.

Chapter 7

Notation

Introduction

From the conclusion that logical properties and relations depend on the internal structures of sentences, Wittgenstein draws the surprising conclusion that conventional logical notation is inadequate: if formal logical properties and relations are there *in* the sentences as they are written, why do we use a notation in which they are not manifest? If one box is bigger than another, then there is an internal relation between them which exists as soon as the two boxes exist, and this relation is manifest and can be seen by looking at the two boxes. But in the case of logic, a similarly internal relation has in most cases to be discovered through calculation, and cannot simply be gathered from looking at the sentences involved. Thus:

The sentences of logic are tautologies. [T 6.1]

If sentences are to yield a tautology when they are connected in a certain way, they must have certain structural properties. So their yielding a tautology when combined *in this way* shows that they possess these structural properties. [T 6.12]

It follows from this that we can actually do without sentences of logic; for in an adequate notation we can actually recognise the formal properties of sentences by mere inspection of the sentences themselves.[1] [T 6.122]

---

[1] The word *entsprechend* is translated here as 'adequate', following Ogden, but the German also has the relevant connotations of corresponding to something, being proportionate to something, and being suitable.

What Wittgenstein proposes—and this is the main point of the present chapter—is that an adequate or perspicuous notation would allow us simply to *see* logical relations between sentences, and in this case there would be no need to go through the process of deducing sentences of logic in a logical system. The consequence is that the whole apparatus of deduction—the axioms, theorems, lemmas, rules, and proofs—would become superfluous in the advent of such an adequate notation. (This explains the subjunctive 'would' in T 5.132.)

Logical relations are internal, so when two sentences are given, their logical relations to one another are thereby also given. Therefore a notation which says what it means in a straightforward and perspicuous way will render these relations manifest. The information is all in the sentences; so if it is not manifest, this must be due to an obscuring notation which encodes and hides the information, with the result that we then have to do the work of decoding it.

The discussion in the *Tractatus* is, or at least tries to be, non-epistemological in character. However the present puzzle is perhaps most persuasively presented in an epistemological vein. As Wittgenstein says:

If p follows from q, the sense of 'p' is contained in the sense of 'q'. [T 5.122]

Thus, if we *knew* the senses of 'p' and 'q', we would know that one is contained in the other, and that one sentence is a logical consequence of the other, without the need for calculation. As it is we do need to calculate, and so it seems that our notation obscures so much that we do not fully know what we mean.

In any case, several notational alternatives are investigated in the *Tractatus*: (1) Russellian notation, (2) Sheffer's stroke, (3) Wittgenstein's Bracket Notation, and (4) his N operator, which generates formal series of sentences. (Wittgenstein's Tabular Notation and Truth-Conditions Notation are also put forward in the *Tractatus* though not in this context.) However, the points Wittgenstein makes are not brought together to form a coordinated discussion, perhaps because his investigation is inconclusive, and does not produce what is desired—a perspicuous notation in which logical properties and relations are manifest.

Russell's Notation

In the Notes on Logic, Wittgenstein had already expressed dissatisfaction with the notation of *Principia Mathematica*:

> If p = not-not-p etc., this shows that the traditional method of symbolism is wrong, since it allows a plurality of symbols with the same sense; and thence it follows that, in analyzing such sentences, we must not be guided by Russell's method of symbolising. [NL, p102; cf NL, p101; N, p93; T 5.43]

The objection here is to synonomy in logical notation: any one sentence has an infinity of logical equivalents. In addition to those produced by negation, which Wittgenstein refers to, there are those produced by disjunction and conjunction—the two idempotent connectives. Thus 'p' = '$p \vee p$' = '$p \vee (p \vee p)$' etc; and again 'q' = '$q \& q$' = '$q \& (q \& q)$' etc. And equivalents are easily produced using the other connectives also. For example:

'p' =

'$(p \vee q) \& (q \supset p)$' =

'$\sim(((p \equiv q) \supset (\sim p \& \sim q)) \& (p \supset (p \equiv q)))$' etc.

Wittgenstein's idea seems to be that what we want to say has a single logical form, but since in Russellian notation it can be expressed using sentences of infinitely many different forms, it follows that these do not give the true logical form of what we are saying. In order to do this it is presumably a necessary condition that a notation is what might be called 'unitary': that it allows only one unique sentential expression of any given proposition.

In the context of supporting the *Grundgedanke*, logical equivalence is appealed to in order to show that operators can 'vanish' (T 5.254). In the present context, the problem is rather that operators can *appear*, without changing the meaning of a sentence.

Wittgenstein's main line of attack on Russellian notation, though, is to the effect that it is not perspicuous—that it obscures logical properties and relations, as is clearly stated in his remarks on Sheffer's Stroke.

Sheffer's Stroke

One of the alternatives to Russellian notation which Wittgenstein puts forward is the use of the single stroke operator for joint denial introduced by H. M. Sheffer.

> When we infer q from $p \lor q$ and $\sim p$, the relation between the sentential forms of '$p \lor q$' and '$\sim p$' is masked, in this case, by our mode of signifying. But if instead of '$p \lor q$' we write, for example, '$p \mid q . \mid .p \mid q$', and instead of '$\sim p$', '$p \mid p$' ($p \mid q$ = neither p nor q), then the inner connection becomes obvious. [T 5.1311]

> Russell's notation does not make internal relations clear. It is not clear in his notation that $p \lor q$ follows from $p . q$. In Sheffer's stroke function the internal relation is made clear. $p \mid q . \mid .p \mid q$ follows from $p \mid p . \mid .q \mid q$. [LN, p57]

The second statement, recorded from a lecture given in Cambridge in 1931, reiterates the idea expressed in the *Tractatus*, though the inferences are different. In both cases the '$\mid$' symbol stands for joint-denial: '$p \mid q$' in Truth-Conditions Notation is '$(FFFT)(p, q)$'. The clearest indication is given of Wittgenstein's dissatisfaction with Russellian notation, but there is no explanation of how the joint-denial symbol effects any improvement.

H.O. Mounce mentions no problems with this, and suggests that Wittgenstein's idea is to 'eliminate the plurality of logical constants, thus bringing logical operations under a single form and representing the inner connections between propositions more perspicuously' (Mounce, 1981, p50). It is true that Wittgenstein seems to have had the idea that reduction to one operator might be helpful, though why this should assist in making notation perspicuous is mysterious. It might be thought that what is expressed by a sentence has a logical form, and that this is better represented by a one-operator notation. This might have some persuasiveness if the resulting notation were unitary, but in the case of Sheffer's Stroke this is not so. For example, a sentence A is equivalent to $A \mid A . \mid .A \mid A$ etc., and so there is no single unique way of expressing a given proposition in this notation; and since this equivalence can be reapplied, there is an infinity of sentences in this notation which express any given truth-function. The important question, though, is whether the result is a perspicuous notation—and plainly it is not. In both cases—the disjunctive syllogism in the first quotation, and '$p \& q$' therefore '$p \vee q$' in the second—the alternative notation fails to make the connection between the sentences manifest, and if anything it is harder in this notation to detect the relation of logical consequence without making a calculation. As Max Black says of the first passage:

> This section is interesting as showing the value that W. attached to a suggestive notation (to a 'suitable geometry of signs' we might say) as displaying internal relations, though one might hope for a more persuasive illustration. [Black, *Companion*, p242]

Nor is there any gain in using the stroke sign, as is now customary, to express alternative denial, where '$p \mid q$' expresses the same as '$(FTTT)(p, q)$' does in Truth-Conditions Notation. Using the stroke operator in this way, we have:

$$\therefore \frac{\begin{array}{c} p \vee q \\ \sim p \end{array}}{q} \quad as \quad \therefore \frac{\begin{array}{c} p|p.|.q|q \\ p|p \end{array}}{q}$$

$$\therefore \frac{p \cdot q}{p \vee q} \quad as \quad \therefore \frac{p|q.|.p|q}{p|p.|.q|q}$$

Here again, there is no increase in the manifestness of the relation of logical consequence—if anything the notation is more rather than less obscure. We cannot see or recognise what relation is involved by mere inspection, and as before we must calculate in order to decode the information concealed in the sentences.

Bracket Notation

In 1913 Wittgenstein had mentioned to Russell the desirability of a notation in which tautologous sentences were recognisable as such— a notation in which they bear their character on their sleeve.

> The great question is now: How should a notation be constructed, which will make every tautology recognisable as a tautology *in one and the same way*? This is the fundamental problem of logic. [LR, p43; cf T 6.1265]

In this letter Wittgenstein suggests the 'ab-notation': this is presented in the *Tractatus* as the Bracket Notation at 6.1203, where 'T' and 'F' replace 'a' and 'b' (cf MN1, p115).

As Black says: 'The method is substantially the same as the more familiar construction and evaluation of truth-tables' (*Companion*, p323). Instead of lining up truth-possibilities and truth-conditions in a tabular manner, these are connected using brackets and lines. This is perhaps best illustrated by displaying the truth-table and the Bracket Notation for the same sentence alongside one another. For example:

'p ∨ q'

p	q	p ∨ q
T	T	T
T	F	T
F	T	T
F	F	F

'p ≡ q'

p	q	p ≡ q
T	T	T
T	F	F
F	T	F
F	F	T

Wittgenstein's best account of the method is given in a letter to Russell:

And this is the *one* symbolic rule: write the proposition down in the *ab*-notation, trace all connection (of poles) from the outside to the inside poles: Then if the *b*-pole is connected to such *groups of inside poles only as contain opposite poles of one proposition*, then the whole proposition is a true, logical proposition. If on the other hand this is the case with the *a*-pole the proposition is false and logical. If finally neither is the case the proposition may be true or false, but is in no case logical. [LR, p36; cf WN, p136]

Using 'T' and 'F' instead of 'a' and 'b', the method is as follows. We trace two outermost poles through to pairs of innermost poles, ignoring the intermediate poles (and thus discovering the truth-conditions of the sentence). We then *discount* any connection between an outermost pole and a pair of different (contradictory) innermost poles attached to the same sentence. If the remaining connections are all to the outermost '*T*', then the sentence is a tautology (it has no falsity-grounds). If they are all to the outermost '*F*', then the sentence is a contradiction (it has no truth-grounds). And if some of the acceptable connections are to the outermost '*T*', and some are to the outermost '*F*', then the sentence is a logical contingency (it has both truth-grounds and falsity-grounds).

What happens in the *Tractatus* is that Wittgenstein simply omits to say this, and the result is an incomplete description of his notation. And without the rule that we discount certain links, the notation cannot be read. This problem arises in the final example in 6.1203, where '$\sim(p.\sim q)$' is translated as:

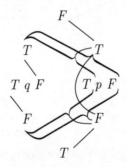

The sentence is tautologous, but in order to see this we need the method of reading the notation given in the letter to Russell.

Max Black's solution to the problem of the 'embarrassing outermost *F*' is to say: 'W. needs a supplementary convention, forbidding the drawing of lines between the positive and negative poles of the same proposition' (*Companion*, p323). The trouble with this idea is that the lines in question would have to appear and disappear according to what we put in for '*p*' and '*q*'. For example, if '*q*' were put in for the '*p*', these lines would have to reappear, despite the fact that the structure of the proposition remains constant. For this reason, Wittgenstein's convention of drawing in these lines and then discounting them seems preferable.

The Bracket Notation is in keeping with Wittgenstein's general project, since the tautologousness, contradictoriness, or contingency of the sentence can be gathered by examining the sentence itself, without the apparatus of a deductive system. But the notation does not satisfy two of Wittgenstein's basic requirements.

First, the Bracket Notation is not unitary. It does allow logical synonomy, just as Russellian notation does, and complex sentences in Bracket Notation can be devised which say the same as simple ones. Just as '$p \lor (p \,\&\, q)$' = 'p', so

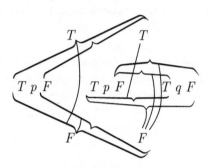

is logically equivalent to

$$T \, p \, F$$

Second, the notation is perspicuous only with respect to the three logical properties of tautologousness, contradictoriness, and contingency. If we have two or more different sentences in Bracket Notation, it is not manifest what logical relations they bear to one another. In the example of two equivalent sentences above, we cannot read the sentences in the manner Wittgenstein describes, and gather that they are equivalent. We could work out the truth-conditions of the sentences by examining them, and then from this determine how they are related, but this would not be in the spirit of what Wittgenstein suggests: it would be a process of calculation. We could also take two sentences in Russellian notation, combine them with '⊃', translate the resulting sentence into Bracket Notation, and then see whether this is a tautology; but again this would be a process of calculation.

Truth-Conditions Notation

Wittgenstein's Truth-Conditions Notation is presented in the context of his Argument from Alternative Notation against the Pictorial View of the logical constants. The question whether it is adequate or perspicuous is not raised, though it actually comes closer to what is required than do the other notational innovations presented in the *Tractatus*.

In Truth-Conditions Notation we simply list the truth-conditions of the sentence, on the understanding that the relevant truth-possibilities are ordered in the manner customary in truth-tables. Thus '$p \supset q$' becomes '$(TFTT)(p, q)$', '$p \equiv q$' is expressed as '$(TFFT)(p, q)$' etc. (see chapter 4). The ordering used here will be Post's rather than Wittgenstein's, the left-hand bracketed part will be called the 'prefix', and the right-hand bracketed part will be called the 'suffix'.

In this notation, the monadic logical properties are certainly manifest: in a tautology the prefix consists only of 'T's, in a logical contingency it consists of a mixture of 'T's and 'F's, and in a contradiction it consists only of 'F's. For example, the tautology '$(p \,\&\, (p \supset q)) \supset q$' is expressed as '$(TTTT)(p, q)$', the contingency '$(p \supset \sim q) \supset (\sim p \supset q)$' is expressed as '$(TTTF)(p, q)$', and the contradiction '$(p \,\&\, q) \,\&\, (\sim p \lor \sim q)$' is expressed as '$(FFFF)(p, q)$'.

The dyadic logical relations are also evident, or at least nearly so. If two sentences in Truth-Conditions Notation are written one above the other, we can compare the 'T's and 'F's and thereby discover what logical relations obtain between them. For example, '$p \,\&\, q$' and '$p \lor q$' in this notation are:

$$(TFFF)(p, q)$$
$$(TTTF)(p, q)$$

If we then follow the rule given by Wittgenstein for logical consequence (T 5.12), we find that it is satisfied: every T in the upper sentence is matched by a 'T' in the lower one. Therefore the upper sentence entails the lower one. (Every truth-possibility which is a truth-ground of the antecedent is also a truth-ground of the consequent.)

One drawback, though, is that this method for reading logical relations will only work when the suffixes of the sentences are the same. The component sentences or sentential variables in the suffixes can easily be arranged in the same order, say alphabetical order, but where the suffixes contain different component sentences, this prevents a straightforward reading. For example, '$(TF)(p)$' and '$(TTTF)(p, q)$' are not commensurable, although the first does entail the second. In such cases, one solution is to construct a second version of the shorter sentence in which the 'T's and 'F's are doubled up so as to make the two commensurable: this then becomes '$(TTFF)(p)$', and then we can see that all its 'T's are matched by 'T's in the other sentence:

$$(TTFF)(p)$$
$$(TTTF)(p, q)$$

However this takes the simplicity out of the method, and the use of an intermediate sentence reduces the extent to which logical relations can simply be read from sentences. And in cases such as '$(\ldots)(p, r)$' and '$(\ldots)(p, q)$', more complex calculation is required.

Truth-Conditions Notation does have another virtue which Wittgenstein does not investigate: so long as the sentence-letters in the suffix are kept in a fixed order, the notation is unitary: any one truth-function can be expressed in only one way. For example, in Russellian notation '$p \supset q$' and '$(p \lor q) \supset q$' are logically equivalent, but of course syntactically different, while in Truth-Conditions Notation, they are both expressed as '$(TFTT)(p, q)$'. As against the infinity of expressions of a given truth-function in Russellian notation, Truth-Conditions Notation, so long as the order in the suffix is kept constant, allows only one.

Truth-Conditions Notation comes closer to perspicuity than do Wittgenstein's other suggested notations, though clearly a degree of calculation is required. Bracket Notation is the only other one which has any degree of perspicuity, but this applies only to the monadic logical properties, and in Truth-Conditions Notation, these are considerably more manifest. And further, in cases where two sentences in Truth-Conditions Notation are commensurable, their logical relations can also be read from the written sentences. There are evidently degrees of calculation and perspicuity: for example, if sentences have prefixes of 16, 32, or more letters, then the process of determining what logical relations hold between them is somewhat less straightforward. But of the alternative notations put forward in the *Tractatus*, Truth-Conditions Notation comes closest to the ideal.

The N Operator

Motivation

Wittgenstein's N operator is the most interesting and the most mysterious of the Tractarian notational innovations. This one operator is to replace the entire symbolic apparatus of the sentential and predicate calculi, and is to provide the 'general sentential form'. It has the fascination of every reduction to essence, and perhaps something of the mood of William Blake's verse:

> To see a World in a Grain of Sand
> And a Heaven in a Wild Flower,
> Hold Infinity in the palm of your hand,
> And Eternity in an hour.

> [Auguries of Innocence, p118]

The motivation for introducing this omnipotent logical symbol is not properly explained in the text of the *Tractatus*: it seems fairest to say that it is not intended to establish any single thesis, but rather to provide a single nail on which to hang a number of existing theses.

The set of all elementary sentences determines a set of truth-functions. These truth-functions allegedly arrange themselves in a series (T 5.1). Sentences expressing these truth-functions are connected by internal logical relations (T 5.131). The mechanical counterpart of an internal relation between two sentences is an operation which takes the first as its base, and produces the second as its result. Representing logical relations in this way somehow 'gives prominence' to them (T 5.21-2). Repeated application of an operation will produce a series ordered by the internal relation which is the counterpart to the operation (T 5.232). Lastly, there is allegedly a single form common to all sentences—the general sentential form—whose counterpart is a single primitive symbol (T 5.471-2, 6).

It will take a good nail to suspend all of these theses, and if it is successful, we must ask what has been achieved. The general idea, in any case, seems to be to minimise the paraphernalia of logic, and to place the centre of gravity in representational discourse with the elementary sentences. The elementary sentences, assisted by only one logical operator, then generate the whole of representational language.

Tractarian analysis would work from ordinary sentences down to elementary sentences, while the N operator would work in the other direction. In both cases, the objective is to establish the 'principle of extensionality'—stated at T 5—that all representational discourse reduces to truth-functions of elementary sentences.

It will be argued below that the N operator's success in this endeavour is variable. The N operator can certainly express any truth-function. However, it does not generate any very natural series, it does not give prominence to internal logical relations, its treatment of generality is questionable, and we are given little reason to think that it provides *the* general sentential form. It is not surprising, then, that while many of the ideas in the *Tractatus* were revived several years later in Wittgenstein's lectures and conversations from 1929 to the mid-1930's, the N operator was not.

It is sometimes suggested that the N operator is somehow or other the essence of the *Tractatus* and that all else is subsidiary. Perhaps the most important thing to realise about the N operator is that it is a technical device which is introduced in order to make *philosophical* points—as is true of the other technical innovations in the *Tractatus*. And what we find is that, with some assistance, the technical device works, but that the relevant philosophical points are not very clearly indicated and not very well served.

Operations, Internal Relations, and the General Sentential Form

In the 5.2's, the notions of an operation, an internal relation, and a formal series are brought together:

> The structures of sentences stand in internal relations to one another. [T 5.2]

> In order to give prominence to these internal relations we can adopt the following mode of expression: we can represent a sentence as the result of an operation that produces it out of other sentences (which are the bases of the operation). [T 5.21]

> The internal relation by which a series is ordered is equivalent to the operation that produces one term from another. [T 5.232]

Negation, logical addition, logical multiplication etc. etc. are operations. [T 5.2341]

Negation, disjunction ('logical addition'), and conjunction ('logical multiplication') are given as examples of operations. For example, in Russellian notation, if we take 'p' and 'q' as our bases, and we take disjunction as our operation, then the result is '$(p \lor q)$'. The results of previous operations may also serve as bases to further operations, and so if we take '$(p \lor q)$' and 'r' as our bases, the operation of conjunction will give the result '$((p \lor q) \,\&\, r)$'.

After these general points about operations in the 5.2's, Wittgenstein introduces the N operator itself in the 5.5's.

Every truth-function is a result of successive applications to elementary sentences of the operation

$$'(---T)(\xi,\ldots)'.$$

This operation negates all the sentences in the right-hand pair of brackets, and I call it the negation of those sentences. [T 5.5]

So instead of '$(---T)(\xi,\ldots)$', I write '$N(\bar{\xi})$'.
$N(\bar{\xi})$ is the negation of all the values of the sentential variable ξ. [T 5.502]

If ξ has only one value, then $N(\bar{\xi}) = \sim p$ (not p); if it has two values, then $N(\bar{\xi}) = \sim p . \sim q$ (neither p nor q). [T 5.51]

The meaning of the N operator is first expressed in the Truth-Conditions Notation of 4.442: however many bases are being operated on, only the last truth-value letter is a 'T', while the others are 'F's. Thus the expression might have been more clearly written as '$(FF\ldots,T)(\xi,\ldots)$'. That is, we have joint negation of all the bases of the operation. The equivalent of '$N(p,q,r,\ldots)$' in Russellian notation is '$\sim p \,\&\, \sim q \,\&\, \sim r \,\&\,\ldots$'. Wittgenstein's symbol *xi*-overbar, '$\bar{\xi}$', refers to all the values of the variable *xi*, 'ξ', and so refers to a set of sentences. This discussion culminates, not in the 5's, but at 6:

The general form of the truth-function is $[\bar{p}, \bar{\xi}, N(\bar{\xi})]$.
This is the general form of the sentence. [T 6]

What this says is that every sentence is a result of successive applications to elementary sentences of the operation $N(\bar{\xi})$. [T 6.001]

Wittgenstein's symbolism indicates that the set of all elementary sentences is the starting set, and the relation between each successive term of the series and the next is that determined by the N operator (cf T 5.2522, 5.501).

The N Operator and its Formal Series

As shown by H. M. Sheffer (1913) the operation of joint denial is actually sufficient to produce sentences expressing any truth-function. For example, '$(p \vee q) \& r$' is equivalent to '$(p \mid q) \mid (r \mid r)$'. Joint-denial alone constitutes an 'adequate set' of logical operations (as does alternative-denial). Now Wittgenstein's N operator is a polyadic form of joint-denial and so is clearly also able to express any truth-function.

The N operator may be sufficiently expressive, but we have to ask whether there is an effective algorithm for applying it to a set of sentences in order to generate all the relevant truth-functions—preferably in a meaningful series. That is, we have to ask what 'successive application' really means in this context. The issue is best illustrated by taking a small base-set, say $\{p, q\}$. Applying N successively, we get $N(p, q)$, $N(N(p, q))$, $N(N(N(p, q)))$ etc. But here the terms which are first, third, fifth etc. in the series are all equivalent, as are those which are second, fourth, sixth etc. As we move along the series we switch from something equivalent to '$\sim p \& \sim q$', to something equivalent to '$p \vee q$', and then back again. Of the sixteen possible truth-functions in this case, we have expressed only two.

Clearly, another way of choosing the bases of the operation has to be found: simply making the application of the operation successive as Wittgenstein suggests will not work. Perhaps the most natural suggestion is that as the operation proceeds, its results should be added to the base-set. For example:

term	base-set	result	equivalent in Truth-Conditions Notation
1	$\{p, q\}$	$N(p, q)$	$(FFFT)(p, q)$
2	$\{p, q, N(p, q)\}$	$N(p, q, N(p, q))$	$(FFFF)(p, q)$
3	$\{p, q, N(p, q), N(p, q, N(p, q))\}$	$N(p, q, N(p, q), N(p, q, N(p, q)))$	$(FFFF)(p, q)$

However, after the second term, the results, although syntactically different, are all equivalent to the second term, which is a contradiction. This is guaranteed, since the members of the base-set $\{p, q, N(p, q)\}$ will be present in the larger base-sets which follow, and whatever else is in a given base-set, these will cause the result to be a contradiction. Thus, we have again only expressed two truth-functions.

If we confine the cumulative base-set to the *results* of the operation, that is if 'p' and 'q' are removed from the base-sets of the second and subsequent terms in the table above, then the repetition begins after the third term, and we express three truth-functions.

What is clear is that these problems will not diminish if we choose a larger base-set, and so they will not disappear if we choose the base-set Wittgenstein proposes—the set of all elementary sentences.

Thus, unless a new and effective algorithm is devised which both dictates how the N operator is to be applied, and allows it to express all truth-functions, we have two options. First, we can retain an algorithm of the sort described above, in which case only a handful of truth-functions are expressed. Or second, we can allow the operator to be applied freely to any members of the cumulative base-set, in which case no unique or meaningful series is produced.

Mounce (1981) and Black (*Companion*) in their discussions seem satisfied with the N operator. Kenny (1973) describes how the N operation can be used to generate all truth-functions of a two-membered set, by allowing it to be freely applied to any members of the cumulative base-set, but does not notice that in this way it fails to produce a unique or useful series. But Anscombe (1963) does suggest a proper algorithm for applying the N operation so as to produce all truth-functions in a predetermined way. Anscombe's idea, essentially, is that as we proceed, (a) we build up a cumulative base-set from the results of applying the operation, (b) we apply the operation to all subsets of this cumulative base-set, (c) we treat these in a systematic order, and (d) when the series would start to repeat, that is to produce logically equivalent results, we bring in a new member of the original base-set of elementary sentences.

However, two problems arise with Anscombe's method. First, although it allows us to generate a unique series, it is not explained in what way this is logically meaningful: it does not for example 'give prominence' to the logical relations among its terms. No reason is given, for example, to think that the third and the seventh, or the fifty-fifth and the ninety-fourth terms bear any particular logical relation to one another, or to think that the seventy-eighth has one or other of the logical properties. And second, although the application of the operation is supposed to be a purely syntactic matter, principle (d) is semantic. That is, in order to see that the series is about to start repeating, we have to determine that it will produce logically equivalent sentences, and to do this we have to work out the meanings of its terms.

Wittgenstein means to bring together the notions of a truth-function, a logical relation, an operation, and a series produced by an operation, and the proposal that truth-functions of elementary sentences can be arranged in a series appears at T 4.45. Apart from the problems already mentioned, the most basic problem is that truth-functions do not *naturally* fall into a series: there is no line along which they naturally fall. At T 5.101 a linear arrangement of the 16 truth-functions of two arguments is given, but this sequence has no specially meaningful order. The 2nd term is entailed by 6th, 7th, 8th, 12th, 13th, 14th, and 16th terms. The 9th term is entailed by the 12th, the 15th and the 16th. None of the terms are equivalent. The 5th contradicts the 12th and the 16th etc. There seems to be no single principle at work here, except that if term A is nearer the top of the schema than term B, then A will have more 'T's than B, or the same number, but not fewer. The logical relations are of course all there, but neither this linear arrangement nor any other seems to give them special prominence or perspicuity. With regard to the relation of logical consequence, for example, truth-functions are naturally arranged in a branching structure, and the attempt to force them into a line is a technical exercise without a useful philosophical result.

The N Operator and Generality

As mentioned above, the N operator can be used to formulate general sentences—those which are usually formulated using the existential and universal quantifiers—indeed it must have this capacity if it is to generate all of representational language. Wittgenstein distinguishes between the truth-functional component and the generality component in quantification, and he proposes to use the N operator to take care of the first, and to use variables ranging over the values of propositional functions to take care of the second, so as to provide a new notation for quantification. Regarding this distinction, Wittgenstein says in the *Tractatus*:

I separate the concept *all* from the truth-function. [5.521]

This does not make his meaning plain, though the problem is not that the English (which is Ogden's) is an inaccurate translation, but rather that the German is elliptical. In a letter to Russell, however, Wittgenstein explains this separation:

I suppose you didn't understand how I separate in the old notation of generality what is in it truth-function and what is purely generality. A general proposition is *a* truth-function of *all propositions* of a certain form. [LR, p73, *Monte Cassino*]

As mentioned in chapter 4, the truth-functional component in universal quantification is conjunction, and that in existential quantification is disjunction, and so the N operator, which can express any truth-function, can clearly take care of this. With regard to generality, what we need is a way of indicating that we are talking about things of a general category, without listing them individually. The N operator takes sentences as its bases, so this is done by using a propositional function to indicate a set of sentences without listing or 'enumerating' the members of the set. An example of a propositional function is 'x is serendipitous', which for the argument 'James' has the value 'James is serendipitous'. Thus if we take the values of a propositional function for all values of its variables, we derive a set of sentences to which the N operator can be applied. This method contrasts with enumeration, and consists, as Wittgenstein puts it, in:

... giving a function fx whose values for all values of x are the sentences to be described. [T 5.501]

Now using the N operator with its capacity for arbitrarily many arguments, and a propositional function to specify these, we can perform quantification with these resources alone, without the use of an explicit quantifier-symbol.

If ξ has as its values all the values of a function fx for all values of x, then $N(\bar{\xi}) = \sim(\exists x)fx$. [T 5.52]

If 'ξ' is a variable ranging over all values of the (propositional) function 'x is serendipitous', and 'x' ranges over the values James, Kerry, and Lambert, then '$\bar{\xi}$' will have as values 'James is serendipitous', 'Kerry is serendipitous', and 'Lambert is serendipitous'. '$\bar{\xi}$' indicates all the values of 'ξ', and so '$N(\bar{\xi})$' says that the three sentences above are all false, that is, that nobody (in the range of 'x') is serendipitous.

This N operator notation for generality is important for Wittgenstein, since it helps to square his extensionality principle that 'A sentence is a truth-function of elementary sentences' (T 5) with the need for general sentences. In the usual notation for the predicate calculus, general and non-general sentences seem quite different, but Wittgenstein's N operator notation brings out his philosophical point that they are not. The difference simply lies in the manner of indicating the bases of the N operator: in the case of general sentences this is done through a propositional function, while in the case of non-general sentences it is done by 'enumeration' (cf Ramsey, *Foundations*, p55). The difference is therefore 'inessential' (T 5.501), and general and non-general sentences are alike in expressing truth-functions of logically atomic sentences.

Wittgenstein's presentation of this idea is very brief, and he does not go on to give further examples of multiply quantified sentences translated into his new notation. However it has been shown by Peter Geach that the notation is expressively complete. In making his case Geach introduces the notation '$\ddot{x} : fx$' to mean the class of sentences determined by the propositional function fx. This innovation, which facilitates the use of the notation, replaces Wittgenstein's '$\bar{\xi}$', but it introduces nothing conceptually new, and so it can be seen as faithful to the text of the *Tractatus*. (See Geach 1981, 1982; cf Fogelin, 1982; Soames, 1983.)

The N operator notation does not, however, dissolve quantification away. It is true that in the new notation there are no explicit quantifier symbols, but, as Fogelin points out, what has happened is that generality now attaches to a variable rather than to a quantifier, and 'Wittgenstein's account of explicit quantification over *objects* turns on an implicit quantification over *propositions*' (Fogelin, 1982, p50; cf Black, *Companion*, pp281–2).

Another point is that the N operator is not unique in its capabilities: as Wittgenstein acknowledges in his letter to Russell from *Monte Cassino* (LR, p73), while the N operator expresses joint denial of arbitrarily many bases, we can achieve the same effect with an operator expressing alternative denial over arbitrarily many bases. This, which we might call the 'A operator', says that not all of its truth-arguments are true. Using Geach's innovation, '$\sim(x)fx$' becomes '$A(\ddot{x}:fx)$', '$(\exists x)fx$' becomes '$A(\ddot{x}:A(fx))$', '$(x)fx$' becomes '$A(A(\ddot{x}:fx))$', '$\sim(\exists x)fx$' becomes '$A(A(\ddot{x}:A(fx)))$' etc. Since the A operator also expresses any truth-function, and since generality can likewise be introduced through propositional functions, its capacities are the same as those of the N operator. In this light, the rôle of the N operator in giving *the* general sentential form becomes less credible. It might be replied that what is given is a *form*, and that it does not matter what truth-conditions attach to whatever is put in the place of the N operator. But then it is not clear what we are being offered, except for the suggestion that we represent generality through a variable rather than a quantifier, and the thought that a single adequate connective will suffice to express all truth-functions.

Summary

From his conclusion that logical properties and relations depend on the internal structures of sentences, Wittgenstein was led to investigate the possibility of a perspicuous notation in which these would be manifest in sentences themselves. In the advent of such a notation the rules of inference and the other apparatus of deductive logic 'would be superfluous'. The information is in there in sentences themselves, and so it should be made accessible, thus relieving us of the need for mechanical assistance in extracting it. The remarks in the *Tractatus* on this subject are scattered and uncoordinated, but they are all aimed at the target of superceding the logic of *Principia Mathematica* with a new method based on a perspicuous notation. In this new notation, seeing would supersede thinking, and perception would replace calculation. The investigation, however, is essentially inconclusive, and it remains the case that while the mirror brightly reflects the world, it obscures its own inner relations.

Of the options which Wittgenstein suggests, Sheffer's Stroke and the N operator notation are not perspicuous. Bracket Notation, when the gap in the account given in the *Tractatus* is filled, is semi-perspicuous with regard to the monadic logical properties, but it does not make dyadic logical relations between sentences manifest at all. The most feasible option is Truth-Conditions Notation, but even this lacks perspicuity where the suffixes of sentences are different.

The most striking of the Tractarian notational innovations is the N operator, whose purposes go beyond the creation of a perspicuous notation, and include the pinning together of various of the Tractarian doctrines on representational language. However, the N operator's effectiveness in this philosophical objective is limited, and its main success is the technical one of providing an alternative notation of the same expressive power as the predicate calculus.

Chapter 8

Other Things Syntactic

Introduction

In addition to assigning logic and identity to the syntactic division, Wittgenstein gives similar, though brief, accounts of probability, modality, the objects of mathematics and scientific theory, and the causes of error in philosophy. His treatments of these topics naturally differ in detail, but what they have in common is their opposition to Naïve Representationalism: in each case he denies that what is under examination is the factual subject matter of a 'science', and assigns it instead to the inside of the great mirror.

Probability

The Tractarian accounts of probability and modality are based on the theory of truth-functions. The treatment of these topics is very brief, and in both cases there is no supporting argument or detailed consideration of similar or alternative views. The Tractarian account of probability is of the 'logical' type, and is similar to the accounts given by Bolzano, Laplace, Keynes, and Carnap, in that it is based on the ratio of the number of favourable to the number of logically possible cases (see Black, *Companion*, pp247–258). The principal remark on probability appears at 5.15:

> If T_r is the number of the truth-grounds of a sentence 'r', and if T_{rs} is the number of the truth-grounds of a sentence 's' that are at the same time truth-grounds of 'r', then we call the ratio $T_{rs}:T_r$

the degree of *probability* that the sentence 'r' gives to the sentence 's'. [T 5.15]

For example, as laid out in the table below, the sentence '$p \lor q$' has three truth-grounds, and it has two truth-grounds in common with the sentence 'p', and so '$p \lor q$' gives to 'p' the probability of 2:3. That is: given the truth of '$p \lor q$', and no other information, it follows that 'p' has a probability of 2:3.

	p	q	$p \lor q$	$T [p \lor q, p]$: $T [p \lor q]$
1	T	T	T	
2	T	F	T	$2/3$
3	F	T	T	
4	F	F	F	

This account of conditional probability gives technical expression to the idea that the first sentence r blocks off certain truth-possibilities (its falsity-grounds), and leaves others open (its truth-grounds). So, on the assumption that the first sentence is true, only those truth-possibilities which are its truth-grounds are left open to the second sentence s. Thus the probability that s is true is dictated by the proportion of these open truth-possibilities which are truth-grounds of s. The first sentence r confines the 'logical space' of truth-possibilities left open to the second sentence s, and so the probability that s is true depends on what proportion of the truth-possibilities in the remaining space make it true.

In the example above '$p \lor q$' leaves open truth-possibilities *1*, *2*, and *3*; and only *1* and *2* make 'p' true; so '$p \lor q$' gives to 'p' the probability of 2:3.

A second example: '$(p \supset q) \& (p \lor q)$' leaves open truth-possibilities *1* and *3*, and '$p \equiv q$' has as truth-grounds truth-possibilities *1* and *4*, and so the second sentence has as truth-grounds one of the two truth-possibilities left open by the first. Hence the first sentence gives to the second a probability of 1:2, which amounts to independence.

A third example: the sentence '$\sim p$' leaves open truth-possibilities *3* and *4*, and '$\sim(p \& q)$' has as its truth-grounds truth-possibilities *2*, *3*, and *4*. So all of the options left open by the first sentence make the second sentence true, and as a result the first gives to the second the probability of 1 (2:2). As Wittgenstein says (T 5.152), in such cases the first sentence entails the second. Indeed, what this probability relation amounts to is an adjustable entailment relation: given n different component sentences, there may be $2^n + 1$ different degrees of relative probability between sentences made up of these components (the number of truth-possibilities plus the zero case).

A minor problem arises when the antecedent in the probability relation is an inconsistency. An inconsistency r has no truth-grounds, and so for any s, $T_{rs} : T_r = 0{:}0$. But the result of dividing any number by zero is undefined, and so $0{:}0$ is undefined. If logical consequence is analysed as tautological implication, as it is in the *Tractatus*, an inconsistency r entails every sentence s, and so where r is an inconsistency, the probability given to any s should be 1. And it seems natural to say that a contradiction entails itself, and thus gives itself a probability of 1, and so in this case in particular the result should be 1. Thus in order to make Wittgenstein's analysis of probability work, and in order to make it cohere with the rest of the *Tractatus*, we must stipulate that $0{:}0 = 1$.

Wittgenstein's account concerns conditional or relative probability, but it can be adapted to absolute probability by taking a tautology as the antecedent in the formula. Thus to determine the probability of '$p \lor q$', we could take '$p \lor \sim p$' as the antecedent, whereupon we have: $T[p \lor \sim p, \, p \lor q] : T[p \lor \sim p] = 3{:}4$.

The philosophical significance of this analysis, within the general scheme of the *Tractatus*, is that since probability is determined by the truth-conditions of sentences, and since these are syntactically determined, probability relations are syntactic rather than factual. Probability relations take their place with the other logical relations such as inconsistency and entailment: they are internal to the sentences they relate and take care of themselves, and they are not relations or 'objects' connecting facts. As Wittgenstein puts it:

There is no special object peculiar to probability statements. [T 5.1511]

In interpreting this remark, Black (*Companion*, p248) takes it to mean that probability statements are *a priori*; but this epistemological point is not what is central to Wittgenstein's case, and it is not what he says. His point is that probability relations are not objects in the world, and that they, like the other logical relations, are internal to sentences in language: being-an-object is contrasted with being-a-syntactic-relation. There are, according to the *Tractatus*, no probability relations between facts, and no second-order triadic probability-facts composed of two facts and a probability relation between them. Probability, like the logical relation of entailment, takes its place inside the great mirror.

Modality

In his remarks on the modalities of necessity, possibility and impossibility, Wittgenstein identifies these with the logical properties of tautologousness, contingency, and contradictoriness respectively:

> The truth of a tautology is certain, that of a sentence possible, and that of a contradiction impossible. [T 4.464]

> It is incorrect to render the sentence '$(\exists x)fx$' in the words, 'fx is *possible*', as Russell does. The certainty, possibility, or impossibility of a situation is not expressed by a sentence, but by an expression's being a tautology, a sentence with a sense, or a contradiction. The precedent to which we are constantly inclined to appeal must reside in the symbol itself. [T 5.525]

In opposition to Russell (see *Logic and Knowledge*, p231) the modalities are dissociated from quantification, and are identified with the three logical properties. 'A is necessary' is to be interpreted as '$\models A$', 'A is possible' is to be interpreted as '$not \models \sim A$', and 'A is impossible' is to be interpreted as '$\models \sim A$'. And since these properties are syntactic and attach to sentences rather than to facts, the modalities are syntactic also. There are no modal facts, only modalities internal to sentences: although sentences may be necessary, possible, or impossible, there are no necessary, possible, or impossible facts.

Thus to discover whether a sentence is necessarily true, we must appeal not to the facts but to 'the symbol itself'. Likewise, if it is possible that a sentence be true, this is because the sentence itself is a logical contingency, and not because the world allows that it may be true. And if it is impossible that a sentence be true, this is because the sentence is inconsistent, and not because of a natural impossibility obtaining in the world. Modalities are not properties of facts, and are not expressed by representational sentences, but are syntactic properties which inhere in sentences themselves. They belong to our representational apparatus, not to the world we represent by means of it.

This view of modality reappears in Wittgenstein's discussion of the philosophy of science in the 6.3's:

> ...outside logic everything is accidental. [T 6.3]

> There is no compulsion making one thing happen because another has happened. The only necessity that exists is *logical* necessity. [T 6.37]

The only modality mentioned here is that of necessity, and in T 6.37 it is that of relative necessity, but the remarks exemplify the view, expressed in the 5.15's, that modality is not factual.

Wittgenstein's general view is clear: modality is shifted from its apparent place in the world of facts, to what he holds to be its proper place in syntax. But there are really two things at issue. First, there is the view belonging to the philosophy of logic that *logical* necessity, possibility and impossibility are syntactic—and here there is a great weight of supporting argument. Second, there is the view belonging to the philosophy of science that there is no natural, factual necessity etc. in the world—and this is simply asserted without supporting argument. What is questionable is the *reduction* of all modality to logical modality, not the account of logical modality itself.

A point of detail is that what is necessary is usually taken to be a special case of what is possible, while on Wittgenstein's account the two are mutually exclusive: if a statement is a tautology then it cannot be a 'sentence with a sense' (in this context a logical contingency). However, Wittgenstein's account can easily be modified to accommodate this point by saying that possibility consists in a sentence's being either a tautology or a logical contingency.

The Tractarian account of modality can be seen as an additional argument in favour of the *Grundgedanke*: from the view that modality belongs to language rather than to the world, it follows that the modal operators are not names of objects in the world. The explicit arguments in favour of the *Grundgedanke* concern the logical connectives, but Wittgenstein's points about the identity-sign, the quantifiers, and modality make the same case for these operators.

On Wittgenstein's view, however, the modal operators differ from these others, since statements in which they appear are about sentences rather than about facts. Although the other operators are not names of objects, they can appear in representational sentences, but the modal operators can only appear in statements about other sentences, since we can only say of *sentences* that they are necessary, possible, or impossible.

Mathematics

A full treatment of the views on mathematics expressed in the *Tractatus*, and of their relation with Wittgenstein's later views, would require an extended discussion. But for present purposes, it is enough to point out that Wittgenstein's general purpose is to give an internal, syntactic account, similar to that given of logic. Wittgenstein starts by saying:

> Mathematics is a logical method. The sentences of mathematics are equations, and therefore pseudo-sentences. [T 6.2]

He says that an equation means that its terms can be substituted for one another, but '... whether this is the case or not must be shown by the two expressions themselves' (T 6.23), and 'this can be seen from the two expressions themselves' (T 6.232). And emphasising that mathematics concerns symbols rather than facts, he says:

> And the possibility of proving the sentences of mathematics means simply that their correctness can be recognised without having to compare what they express with facts in order to determine its correctness. [T 6.2321]

The subject matter of mathematics is syntactic rather than factual: the relation of inter-substitutability, or synonomy, of two expressions in mathematics is grounded in the expressions themselves— so long as the meanings of the constituent terms are given—and does not depend on anything external. Equations are therefore non-representational: the point of saying that they are 'pseudo-sentences' is not that they are vacuous or erroneous, but that, although they may seem to be fact-stating, they are not. (With regard to the similarity between Wittgenstein's views of mathematics and logic,

T 6.232 is comparable with T 6.113 which gives the 'whole philosophy of logic', and T 6.2321 is comparable with T 5.551 which gives his 'fundamental principle'.)

Scientific Theory

The philosophy of science is discussed in the 6.3's in the *Tractatus*, where Wittgenstein's concern is with scientific laws and theories, rather than with the individual statements about the world which he calls 'sentences of science'. On what might be called a 'Representational View' of statements of scientific laws and theories, these might be thought to state natural, causal necessities, to give explanations of natural phenomena, and to describe the world of facts: it might be thought that all that differentiates them from ordinary representational statements is that they describe general and necessary aspects of the world, as opposed to individual and contingent facts.

What Wittgenstein does is to attack this Representational View from various angles, and to replace it with the theses (*1*) that there are no natural necessities to be described anyway, and (*2*) that the rôle of scientific laws and theories is the non-representational one of providing *forms* of description, which in turn are used to cast the sentences which do represent the world.

Thesis (*1*) is the Tractarian account of modality, discussed above: natural necessity is dismissed with the statement that 'The only necessity is *logical* necessity' (T 6.37; cf T 6.3; N, p41). The absence from the world of logical necessity is of course established by the Logical Independence Thesis, but argument is not provided in the *Tractatus* to establish that all putative forms of natural or worldly necessity actually reduce to something logical.

Thesis (*2*) is given more extended argument, for example:

The law of causality is not a law but the form of a law. [T 6.32]

All such statements, including the principle of sufficient reason, the laws of continuity in nature and of least effort in nature etc. etc.—all these are *a priori* insights about the forms in which the sentences of science can be cast. [T 6.34; cf N, p42]

And following his analogy between a scientific theory and a grid or net, he says:

> Laws like the principle of sufficient reason etc. are about the net and not about what the net describes. [T 6.35]

Thus, scientific laws concern syntax rather than facts: the world is not described by such scientific principles, but by what they provide us with. By analogy, a die for stamping metal cups for drinking is not itself used for drinking—rather it is a stamp which gives the form of cups, and it is the cups it provides us with which are used for drinking. The mistake Wittgenstein means to put right is analogous to that of confusing the function of the die with the function of the cups whose form it provides. Just as Logic is about sentences rather than what they describe, so the laws cited are about the 'net' of representational language rather than the world which the net describes.

Wittgenstein's view is reminiscent of Kant, in the *Critique of Pure Reason*, according to whom various of what might be thought to constitute external necessities are actually regulative principles of the mind *through which* we conceive the world. And Wittgenstein's view on the subject matter of scientific theory is analogously that what may appear to be necessary aspects of the world are actually aspects of the linguistic forms through which we represent the world. Although Wittgenstein's view is linguistic while Kant's is conceptual, a similarity in spirit can be seen; and in both cases there is an injunction against projection onto the world of what properly belongs to our mode of representing or conceiving it.

Wittgenstein's concern in the 6.3's is mostly to place this category of seemingly representational statements into the non-representational division, but in the case of the 'law of induction' his purpose is the opposite:

> The so-called law of induction cannot possibly be a law of logic, since obviously it is a sentence with a sense.—Nor, therefore, can it be an *a priori* law. [T 6.31]

The law of induction is the principle that future events will conform to those of the past: this attributes regularity to the world, and so is representational. It seems unfair here to take him to be making the obvious point that the law of induction is not a tautology of formal logic: rather his point seems to be that, like the Axiom of Reducibility (T 6.1232), the law of induction, despite its appearance, is representational. Wittgenstein has a habit of using the name of one member of a type to refer to the members of that type—for example he uses 'space' to indicate determinables in general—and here he uses 'logic' loosely to refer in general to what is syntactic, necessary, and accessible *a priori*.

The view of scientific theory put forward in the *Tractatus* agrees with that of Hertz in allowing for representational diversity: different representational forms can be used to describe the world. At T 6.341, Wittgenstein draws an analogy between the rôle of scientific theory and that of a net or grid: a white surface with irregular black patches on it is described by covering it with a regular network, and then saying of each cell whether it is black or white, and in this way we have 'imposed a unified form on the description of the surface'. Wittgenstein then says that 'The form is optional, since I could have achieved the same result by using a net of triangular or hexagonal mesh'. Thus, although a scientific system such as Newtonian mechanics 'imposes a unified form on the description of the world', alternative forms of representation may be used.

Representational diversity was one of Hertz's central concerns: he held that the same 'system' may have several 'dynamical models'. As he put it at one point: 'Various images of the same objects are possible, and these images may differ in various respects' (*Principles of Mechanics*, p2). However, Hertz rejects as inadmissible any 'image' which contradicts the 'laws of our thought' or the 'relations of external things'; and he says that of two admissible images, the one which is simpler and which 'pictures more of the essential relations of the object' (*loc cit*) is to be preferred. Thus, according to Hertz, the choice of forms of representation is not arbitrary, and among those forms which are viable some are more informative than others.

This is a crucially important issue, but Wittgenstein says very little about it. A wedge has been driven between the factual and the syntactic, and the question is whether it has parted them entirely. It seems evident that an extreme representational relativism would be incorrect—one representational system is not as good as another. Wittgenstein does suggest, like Hertz, that representational systems can vary in *comprehensiveness, simplicity* and *accuracy* of description (T 6.341-1), but does not in literal terms say why this is so. The general point seems to be that although a representational system *says* nothing about the world—it tells us no facts—it must nevertheless be somehow *commensurate* with its factual subject matter. The issue is important for the evaluation of the products of all the disciplines which, according to the *Tractatus*, deal with syntax. Since representational systems vary in value, intra-syntactic work in philosophy, logic etc. can—like work in scientific theory—be in part assessed according to whether it allows greater simplicity, accuracy, and comprehensiveness of description—this being what makes alteration of the net worthwhile.

In any case, Hertz's held that representational forms do say something about the world, since they are capable of contradicting the 'relations of external things', and some forms picture more of the 'essential relations of the object' than others. Wittgenstein does, very briefly, consider the question:

> The laws of physics, with all their logical apparatus, nevertheless speak, however indirectly, about the objects of the world. [T 6.3431]

Discussing the analogy of the net, Wittgenstein says:

> And now we can see the relative position of logic and mechanics. (The net might also consist of more than one kind of mesh: for example we could use both triangles and hexagons.) The possibility of describing a picture like the one mentioned above with a net of a given form tells us *nothing* about the picture. (For that is true of all such pictures.) But what *does* characterise the picture is that it can be described *completely* by a particular net with a *particular* size of mesh.

> Similarly the possibility of describing the world by means of Newtonian mechanics tells us nothing about the world: but what does tell us something about it is the precise *way* in which it is possible to describe it by these means. We are also told something about the world by its being described more simply by one system of mechanics than by another. [T 6.342]

The 'picture' here is the white surface with irregular black patches, and Wittgenstein's point is that although we are told nothing about the world by the admissibility of a particular form of representation, its capacity to provide a *complete* description does tell us something about the world. The distinction is drawn here between what is said about the world by a form of representation itself—nothing—and what is said by the additional statement that that particular form of representation can provide a complete description of the world—presumably a great deal.

To follow Wittgenstein's analogy of the net, it might be, for example, that the net used consisted of exactly circular cells, and that no complete description of the surface resulted unless an infinitesimally fine mesh were used (as would happen if the black patches were exactly square). In this case the nature of the net together with its being unsuitable for describing the surface would tell us something about the surface: that the black patches were not circular, or of such a shape as can be represented by a combination of circles. If, however, the net consisted of square cells, and a complete description resulted, this would tell us that the black patches were of such a shape and size as to be covered exactly by patterns of these squares, and also that the black patches were right-angled. And if an alternative net of smaller square cells resulted in a complete but more complex description, we could again conclude something about the surface described. It is thus at least an exaggeration to say as Wittgenstein does that 'the form is optional' (T 6.341), since the form of the mesh determines the simplicity of description provided, and also whether or not a complete description is possible at all.

That a particular net provides a complete description of the surface, then, does tell us something about the surface, but this is an empirical, contingent matter. The net itself does not say anything about the surface: as Wittgenstein puts it 'The network, however, is *purely* geometrical; all its properties can be given *a priori*' (6.35). And similarly, he holds that it is an empirical, contingent matter whether or not the representational form given by a scientific theory provides a complete description of the world—the necessary and *a priori* element in scientific theory attaches to the form of representation itself, and not to what it is used to represent.

A consequence of Wittgenstein's non-representational view of scientific laws is that they are not *explanations* of the workings of the physical world as might be supposed on a Representational View (T 6.371; cf N, p72). On this point he says:

Thus people today stop at the laws of nature as at something unas-
sailable, as people in the past did with God and Fate. [T 6.372]

As is made clear in Wittgenstein's letters to Ogden (LO, p35),
Wittgenstein's meaning is that there is an erroneous tendency to
think that once we have the laws of nature we have a satisfactory
explanation of the world, whereas they are really not explanations
at all.

Wittgenstein's view is that the true subject matter of scientific
theory is syntactic rather than factual: a system such as Newton's
or Hertz's mechanics does not describe the world, but provides a
form of representation with which representational 'sentences of science' can be formulated. A system of mechanics is at two removes
from the world, and the *a priori* and necessary elements which are
to be found in such a system are not pictorial—they are internal to
the form of representation and do not represent natural necessities.
Max Black suggests that scientific theory constitutes a problem case
for Wittgenstein's theory of meaning, and that none of the scientific principles considered in the 6.3's 'fit snugly into any of the slots
so far provided in Wittgenstein's theory of meaning' (*Companion*,
p334). On the contrary, although scientific theory might constitute
a problem for a Naïve Representationalist, Wittgenstein's scheme
is more sophisticated and accommodates the case quite naturally.
Rather than being a peculiarly problematic type of discourse, scientific theory is one of a series of cases to which Wittgenstein gives
similar treatment.

It is hard to assess whether Wittgenstein is right in what he says,
since what is given in the *Tractatus* is an outline rather than a fully
developed philosophy of science. It is problematic that reason is not
given for the dismissal of all natural necessity; and it is unfortunate
that the word 'logical' is used loosely to refer to the syntactic, without stipulating exactly what is at issue. A further difficulty is that
of determining to which scientific laws and principles Wittgenstein's
analysis is applicable. The cases Wittgenstein discusses all involve
universal generalisation, but it is left unclear whether this is to be
the criterion by which to differentiate representational 'sentences of
natural science' from non-representational scientific laws.

A source of strong appeal, though, in Wittgenstein's account is its
explanation of the *a priori* element in natural science. Any variation
of the Representational View has to deal with the epistemological

problem of explaining how we come to know universal or even necessary truths about the world on the basis of observations which are limited in number, space, and time. But on Wittgenstein's account, since our access to syntax is less limited than our access to the world, the problem does not arise.

Philosophy

When Wittgenstein turns to the question of the nature of philosophical discourse itself, his answer, as so often in the *Tractatus*, is that it is non-representational. Against this background, three different views of the nature of philosophical discourse can be discerned, which I shall call the 'Demarcation Model', the 'Therapy Model', and the 'Nonsense Model': these do not coalesce to form a single coherent picture, but they do have in common the idea that philosophy is not a representational, fact-stating 'science'.

Science, as usually conceived, is an organised activity conducted by serious people in white coats, but for Wittgenstein it is the totality of representational language:

> The totality of true sentences is the whole of natural science (or the whole corpus of the natural sciences). [T 4.11]

And a 'sentence' is not just any statement, but a representational one which fits with his account of fact-stating language:

> A sentence represents the existence and non-existence of elementary facts. [T 4.1]

Wittgenstein confines the usual meaning of 'sentence', extends the usual meaning of 'science', and states that philosophy is not a (representational) science producing (representational) sentences. Thus:

> Philosophy is not one of the natural sciences. [T 4.111]

> Philosophy is not a body of doctrine but an activity. Philosophy does not result in 'philosophical sentences' ... [T 4.112]

This view is anticipated in the 'Notes on Logic' of 1913:

Philosophy gives no pictures of reality. Philosophy can neither confirm nor confute scientific investigation (NL, p106).

And it is later echoed in the *Philosophical Investigations*:

It was true to say that our considerations could not be scientific ones ... And we may not advance any kind of theory. There must not be anything hypothetical in our considerations ... These are, of course, not empirical problems; they are solved, rather by looking into the workings of our language ... [PI, §109]

Philosophy, then, is not a 'science', and does not result in 'sentences', 'doctrines', or 'hypotheses'—it is not fact-stating. To science has been assigned the rôle of describing the world of facts, and philosophy is excluded from assisting in this task. Wittgenstein's target is Naïve Representationalism—here the view that philosophy, like natural science, is concerned with facts, albeit facts of a special general, abstract, eternal or platonic sort. And in true Tractarian style, it is argued that rather than being concerned with special facts, we are not concerned with facts at all.

These views were formulated in reaction to Russell who had argued that philosophy is the most general of the sciences, differing in degree rather than kind from her overtly empirical sisters, and using formal logic as her tool. And Russell's beliefs on the nature of philosophy no doubt constituted an important 'centre of repulsion' for Wittgenstein's views (see Baker and Hacker, 1980, p260; cf Russell 1914, and Russell 1918). As usual, though, Wittgenstein's views constitute more than just the negations of various theses he disagreed with: they carry their own perspective, and must be examined in their own terms.

The Demarcation Model

Against the general background of a non-representationalist conception of philosophy, the *Tractatus* contains, as already mentioned, three distinct conceptions.

According to the Demarcation Model, philosophy's rôle is to differentiate between the inhabitants of the categories in the Tractarian scheme—in particular to differentiate representational discourse ('science') from non-representational discourse. Thus:

Philosophy demarcates the boundary of the controversial domain
of natural science. [T 4.113]

In a letter written to Russell, Wittgenstein's said of the *Tractatus*:

> The main point is the theory of what can be expressed (gesagt)
> by propositions—that is by language—(and, which comes to the
> same thing, what can be *thought*) and what can not be expressed
> by propositions, but only shown (gezeigt) ; which, I believe, is
> the cardinal problem of philosophy. [LR, p71; Monte Cassino,
> 19.8.1919]

And later, in the early 1930's, a trace of the same view was recorded
in Moore's lecture notes: Wittgenstein said that the 'new subject'
(his programme in philosophy) consisted in 'something like putting
in order our notions as to what can be said about the world' [MN2,
p323].

Wittgenstein's idea here is straightforward, though his terminology is not, and Black (*Companion*, p187) rightly calls T 4.113 'an
obscure remark'. We are told that philosophy differentiates what
belongs to 'natural science' and can be 'said' about the 'world' from
what does not so belong and can only be 'shown': that is, it differentiates representational from non-representational discourse.

This is not intended as the legalistic judgement of what constitutes a semantic trespass, but as the investigation of a central issue
in the theory of representation. The view is certainly true of the
Tractatus itself, since just such a demarcation is undertaken there.
However, the effect of the *Tractatus* is clearly more sophisticated,
since it also differentiates the nonsensical from the non-representational (and the mystical from the syntactic).

The Therapy Model

According to the Therapy Model, philosophy has the rôle of curing
certain linguistic ailments—in particular confusion engendered by
the superficial grammatical forms of the sentences we use.

As presented in the 4.1's this seems to be the rather bland thesis
that philosophy is an activity of clarification: the activity of making
what we say and think more perspicuous and distinct. We are told

at T 4.112 that philosophy consists in the 'clarification' and 'elucidation' of thoughts and sentences which are otherwise 'cloudy and indistinct'.

However Wittgenstein did have something more specific and much more interesting in mind, though ironically this is not very clearly expressed. The idea is anticipated in the 'Notes on Logic' where he says:

> Distrust of grammar is the first requisite of philosophising. (NL, p106)

And in the 3.23's in the *Tractatus* he remarks briefly on the reasons for this distrust:

> In everyday language it very frequently happens that the same word has different modes of signification ... or that two words that have different modes of signification are employed in sentences in what is superficially the same way. Thus the word 'is' figures as a copula, as a sign for identity, and as an expression for existence; 'exists' figures as an intransitive verb like 'go', and 'identical' as an adjective; we speak of *something*, but also of *something's* happening. [T 3.323]

> In this way the most fundamental confusions are easily produced (the whole of philosophy is full of them). [T 3.324]

The discussion in the *Tractatus* is brief, but the idea expressed is perhaps the most important of Wittgenstein's metaphilosophical ideas, and reappears in his later writings. And the solution which is suggested at this point in the *Tractatus*, that of a logically perfect language (see T 3.325), is clearly not an end to the matter.

Two types of grammatically-generated confusion are identified at T 3.323. The first might be called the 'Fallacy of Univocity': a single word may have various meanings, and, as Wittgenstein later came to think, the things falling under a word may be connected not by a single common factor but by overlapping 'family resemblances'. Thus if, ignoring context, we treat a word as if it did have a single unitary meaning, confusion results. The second problem might be called the 'Fallacy of Grammatical Analogy': confusion results if we assume that words which play the same grammatical rôle in sentences are therefore similar in the sorts of things they signify. Wittgenstein's point in both cases is that it is wrong to assume that grammatical cognates are thereby semantic cognates: from the syntactic circumstance that two words are the same (that they are tokens of the same word-type), or that two words have the same grammatical rôle, it does not follow that they are alike in what they signify.

This line of thought naturally involves a distinction between the superficial (and potentially misleading) form of a sentence, and its true 'logical' form. At one point Wittgenstein says:

> Language disguises thought. So much so, that from the outward form of the clothing it is impossible to infer the form of the thought beneath it ... [T 4.002]

This is very reminiscent of Hertz, who had written:

> ...scientific accuracy requires of us that we should in no wise confuse the simple and homely figure, as it is presented to us by nature, with the gay garment which we use to clothe it. Of our own free will we can make no change whatever in the form of the one, but the cut and colour of the other we can choose as we please. [*Electric Waves*, p28]

At 4.0031, Wittgenstein credits Russell with having made the distinction between the 'apparent logical form' of a sentence and its 'real one'. And it is certain that in these thoughts, Wittgenstein was influenced by Russell. When they started their discussions in Cambridge, Russell had already developed the idea that logic can be used as a tool in *analysis* which takes us from the potentially misleading and defective surface form of a sentence to its real 'logical' form. This view crystallised in Russell's Theory of Descriptions (Russell,1905; and Whitehead and Russell's *Principia Mathematica*), and it continued to inform his later work (Russell, 1914; 1918–19). This approach to philosophy in general became a primary theme in the analytical philosophy of the 1930's which Wittgenstein in turn influenced (see for example Ryle, 1931–32). Despite the technicality of his early work, though, Wittgenstein was not one of those who thought that translation into the predicate calculus is enough to solve or dissolve a philosophical problem.

The Therapy Model is not investigated in detail in the *Tractatus*, but it does reappear in the later writings. For example, an analysis of a case of the Fallacy of Grammatical Analogy is given in *Zettel*:

Socrates to Theatetus: 'If you have an idea, must it not be an
idea of *something*?'—Theatetus: 'Necessarily'.—Socrates: 'And if
you have an idea of something, mustn't it be of something real'—
Theatetus: 'It seems so'. If we put the word 'kill', say, in place
of 'have an idea of' in this argument, then there is a rule for the
use of this word: it makes no sense to say 'I am killing something
that does not exist'. I can imagine a stag that is not there, in this
meadow, but not kill one that is not there. And 'to imagine a stag
in this meadow' means to imagine *that* a stag is there. But to kill
a stag does not mean to kill *that* ... [*Zettel*, §69]

The expression 'have an idea of' has a grammatical rôle similar to
that of 'kill', 'eat', 'buy', 'discover' etc.—with the result that these
words can be substituted for it in Socrates' sentence while preserving
its grammatical structure. But the fallacy consists in inferring from
this that the meaning of 'have an idea of' is of the same general
sort as attaches to its grammatical cousins: it consists in assuming
that since these require that a real existing thing should be their
object, the same is true of the original expression. And by observing
that a fallacy has been committed, we avoid the confusion which
results from it—we avoid the erroneous philosophical doctrine that
everything we think of exists. The idea appears in the *Philosophical
Investigations*:

> Our investigation is therefore a grammatical one ... Misunderstandings
> concerning the use of words, caused, among other things, by cer-
> tain analogies between forms of expression in different regions of
> language. [PI, §90]

And again:

> It is not in practical life that we encounter philosophical problems
> (as we may encounter scientific problems)—it is when we start
> constructing sentences not for practical purposes but under the
> influence of certain analogies in language. [Big Typescript 427;
> quoted by A. Kenny in B. McGuinness, ed., *Wittgenstein and his
> Times*]

The Therapy Model, like the other two models, gives detail to
Wittgenstein's general non-representational conception of philosophy. We might see philosophy as being close to natural science:

divorced from the laboratory, to be sure, but nevertheless concerned with facts of some abstract, special sort. And again, we might see philosophy as being concerned with a *second world*, such as Plato's realm of Forms—a reality distinct from the empirical world, but nevertheless comprising representable facts. Both of these conceptions take philosophy to be different from, but analogous to, a representational, fact-oriented science. But Wittgenstein's view is more radical. Philosophy is not a special division of natural science, nor is it a sister discipline concerned with an alternative domain of facts: *in philosophy we do not use our representational apparatus to describe facts of any sort, rather we focus on our representational apparatus itself, and attempt to dissolve illusions generated by misinterpreting it.* The philosopher does not use a special microscope to look at the empirical world, nor a special telescope to look at another world, rather he or she is concerned with the patterns in the eye itself.

The Nonsense Model

According to the third Tractarian conception of philosophy, philosophical discourse is nonsense, and altogether lacks informative content. Thus:

> Most of the statements and questions to be found in philosophical works are not false but nonsensical. Consequently, we cannot give any answer to questions of this kind, but can only establish that they are nonsensical. [T 4.003; cf 6.53].

What Wittgenstein says here concerns the writings of traditional philosophers, rather than philosophy written in the spirit of his own language-oriented programme. The misleading nature of the superficial characteristics of language is the cause, nonsense is the disease, and Wittgenstein's new programme is to be the cure. As Moore records, Wittgenstein distinguished between traditional philosophy and his own:

> He said that what he was doing was a 'new subject', and not merely a stage in a 'continuous development'; that there was now, in philosophy, a 'kink' in the 'development of human thought', comparable to that which occurred when Gallileo and his contemporaries invented dynamics ... [MN2, p322]

So far the Nonsense Model fits comfortably with the other models: nonsensical philosophy is what is cured by the legitimate therapeutic programme of the new philosophy.

However, at the end of the *Tractatus* we find the infamous statement that the *Tractatus* itself comprises nonsense:

> My statements serve as elucidations in the following way: anyone who understands me eventually recognises them as nonsensical, when he has used them—as steps—to climb up beyond them ... [1][T 6.54]

It would be a mistake to pretend that this brief and dramatic statement is easy to interpret, or to pretend that it fits in easily with Wittgenstein's other metaphilosophical views. I would suggest, though, that it is essentially a reaction to an important fault in the *Tractatus*—a point where the book contains the seeds of its own destruction. The problem is that there is no place in the Tractarian scheme for the *Tractatus* itself. In the neat division between fact-stating, non-representational, and nonsensical discourse, there is no place for Wittgenstein's own statements. The Tractarian ontology concerns the ultimate nature of the factual world, but has an *a priori* character incompatible with truly fact-stating discourse. The statements about truth-functionality and the relation between language and the world are yet harder to classify, and so on. But we can hardly believe that the whole lot belongs to the nonsensical division, since true nonsense is uninformative and tells us nothing whatsoever, which is untrue of the *Tractatus*.

Wittgenstein's scrupulousness, for example in avoiding directly talking *about* the mystical, is not really enough to avoid the problem. And simply to say that the statements which comprise the book are nonsense is neither a fair presentation of the problem, nor an adequate answer to it. The problem lies at the heart of the *Tractatus*, and is in effect the problem that the book constitutes a counterexample to its own classification of discourse. To say that the *Tractatus* constitutes nonsense is an attempt to solve the problem within the book's existing classificatory scheme, whereas what is needed is the transcending of that scheme itself.

---

[1]The statement is reminiscent of Sextus Empiricus, 1933–49, Book VIII, p481.

Discussion

In approaching Wittgenstein's early metaphilosophy, we have to deal with statements which are very brief, which are distributed through the *Tractatus*, which are often better explained and amplified in his later writings, and which do not form a wholly coherent picture. Nevertheless, we can discern a clearly non-representational conception of philosophy, against which three more detailed views appear.

Of the relations between the three models of philosophy, perhaps most interesting is the relation between the Therapy Model and the Demarcation Model. The presentation of the Therapy Model relies on the distinction made in the Demarcation Model, and more generally in the Tractarian scheme, between the factual and the syntactic. More strikingly, the errors engendered by the Fallacy of Grammatical Analogy, and which are to be cured by philosophical therapy, are often errors of demarcation within the Tractarian scheme. The *Grundgedanke* in particular can be seen as the denial of such a case of this fallacy: the logical constants are grammatically similar to relational expressions naming real relations, but as it happens the similarity is merely syntactic, and the logical constants do not actually name real relations in the world. The *Grundgedanke* is fundamental to the Tractarian conception of logic, but in a metaphilosophical context it may also have been fundamental to Wittgenstein as a powerful example of the generation of a mistaken *philosophical* view through the Fallacy of Grammatical Analogy.

To this extent, the *Tractatus* is true to its own metaphilosophy. The tendency opposed through much of the book is Naïve Representationalism, and this tendency may often derive appeal from the Fallacy of Grammatical Analogy. The problem is just that discourse which is not about the factual world looks much like discourse which is, and if we assume that the similarity is more than grammatical, we end up as Naïve Representationalists.

The statements 'it is probable that p' and 'q is a logical consequence of r' are grammatically similar to 'it is disastrous that p' and 'q is a distant cousin of r' respectively, but Wittgenstein's case is that the relations of probability and logical consequence, unlike being-disastrous and being-a-distant-cousin-of, do not obtain in the world. The sentences '$a = b$' and 'all events have causes' look like 'a owns b' and 'all radios have batteries', though according to the *Tractatus* the similarity is merely grammatical. The sentence 'x is morally good' looks like 'x is mechanically satisfactory' etc. In each case the grammatical rôle of the key words is similar to that of words which name entities, properties, or relations existing in the world of facts. The tendency which is opposed in much of the *Tractatus* is that of collapsing the syntactic and the mystical into the world of facts, and it seems fair to say that grammatical analogies can add implicit credibility, if not sound and explicit support, to such views. Naïve Representationalism has in the Fallacy of Grammatical Analogy a subtle ally, if not a noisy supporter.

Wittgenstein's remarks on the nature of philosophy have a tremendous ring to them, but they often leave it unclear what is meant. We are told that philosophical problems arise 'because the logic of our language is misunderstood' (T, Preface, p3; cf 4.003), that much traditional philosophy is 'nonsense' (T 4.003), that 'all philosophy is a "critique of language"' (T 4.0031), that philosophy is not a 'natural science' (T 4.111), that it results in 'clarification', that it is an 'activity' (T 4.112), and so on.

However, as Anscombe put it, his remarks 'often turn out to be quite straightforward, and by no means so oracular or aphoristic as they have been taken to be' (*Introduction*, p19). And I suggest that what is essential to making sense of the Tractarian metaphilosophy is to focus, first, on the Tractarian conceptual scheme, second, on the general opposition to Naïve Representationalism, and, third, on the Fallacy of Grammatical Analogy.

Summary

Logic, identity, probability, necessity, possibility, the objects of mathematics and scientific theory, and the causes of philosophical error are all assigned to the syntactic category. These are not things which we represent, but aspects of our representational systems themselves. They are not reflected in the great mirror, but are parts of the mechanism of reflection. They belong not to the world, but to language.

All of the topics which the *Tractatus* assigns to the syntactic category have at first sight a difference in kind from facts in the world—epistemic access to them is *a priori*, and they seem to involve truth of a necessary, universal, eternal character. A law of logic, for example, is discovered in the head rather than in the laboratory, and having discovered it, we do not expect it to hold at some times and in some places, but not others. Naïve Representationalism makes these qualities essential to the special character of these things: in its empirical variety, it assigns them to a special place in the world as we know it; and in its platonic variety it assigns them to a second world populated only by such special facts. Thus philosophy and logic can be seen as studying the most general of facts, mathematics can be seen as studying platonic facts, and so on. On the Tractarian account, though, these qualities are not essential—they are *consequences* of being syntactic.

Naturally, Wittgenstein is not concerned to make *exactly* the same points in each case. The discussion of scientific theory emphasises points which the others do not, and the treatment of philosophical discourse is involved and perhaps the least typical. Nevertheless, the similarity between the Tractarian accounts of these several topics is so great that it would be a travesty of the work to ignore it. And once the common theme of this part of the *Tractatus* is identified, its resonances become clear also—two examples being the theory of mental representation in cognitive science, and the abstractionist movement in visual art (see epilogues I and II).

Although the Tractarian treatment of the syntactic is coherent, it does lack detail in explaining exactly what it is to be syntactic. In general, more attention is given to banishing the various topics from the world of facts than is given to locating them exactly in the syntactic realm, and to explaining just what it is to be an intra-syntactic feature or relation. What is clear, though, is the Tractarian perspective: the middle passages of the *Tractatus* constitute an essay in non-representation, and address the inner features and relations of the great mirror of linguistic representation.

Part IV

BEHIND THE MIRROR

Chapter 9

The Mystical

Wittgenstein's View

In venturing behind the great mirror, the *Tractatus* acquires a breadth of vision uncommon in the philosophy of language. The first sections of the book concern the reflection of the world in the mirror, the middle sections address the inside of the mirror, and now at the end we find remarks on the 'mystical' domain of what lies behind the mirror and cannot be reflected in it. To this last division Wittgenstein assigns the 'sense of the world', value, ethics, aesthetics, the 'problems of life', the revelation of God, and what is 'higher' (T 6.41–6.421, 6.432, 6.52–6.522). These things—which he tends to group under the title of 'ethics'—are not to be found *in* the world: they cannot be represented by 'sentences', and the attempt to put them into words results in nonsense.

The discussion of the mystical in the *Tractatus* is brief, and although the essentials of Wittgenstein's view are given there, useful supplements are provided by the 'Lecture on Ethics' and by Waismann's records of his conversations with Wittgenstein. As Wittgenstein put it in his 'Lecture on Ethics':

> Our words used as we use them in science, are vessels capable only of containing and conveying meaning and sense, *natural* meaning and sense. Ethics, if it is anything, is supernatural and our words will only express facts; as a teacup will only hold a teacup of water if you pour a gallon over it. [LE, p7]

Although the meaning of the passage is clear, the metaphor of the teacup is not ideal, since the inadequacy of a teacup concerns

151

the *quantity* rather than the type of what it can hold. It might be better to say that a sieve (language), which will hold some things (facts), will not hold water (the ethical). The ethical is distinguished from the factual: it does not exist in the world of facts, but outside it:

> Ethics so far as it springs from the desire to say something about the ultimate meaning of life, the absolute good, the absolute[ly] valuable, can be no science. [LE, p11–12]

> Everything I describe is within the world. An ethical sentence never occurs in the complete description of the world, nor even when I am describing a murder. What is ethical is not an elementary fact. [WN, p117; cf N, pp51, 53, and 77–80; and Englemann, 1969]

It might be thought that:

> ... what we mean by saying that an experience has absolute value *is just a fact like other facts* and that all it comes to is that we have not yet succeeded in finding the correct logical analysis of what we mean by our ethical and religious expressions ... [LE, p11]

But according to Wittgenstein, the difficulty of expression and analysis goes deeper, since:

> I see now that these nonsensical expressions are not nonsensical because I had not yet found the correct expressions, but that their nonsensicality was their very essence. [LE, p11]

To attempt to describe the ethical is to 'run against the boundaries of language' (LE, p12): something akin to the Kantian *hubris* of extending Reason beyond its limits. Since the ethical is intrinsically indescribable, the attempt to describe it results in nonsense, and no sound analysis can turn nonsense into sense.

Here, as in the *Tractatus*, Wittgenstein uses the expressions 'world', 'sentence', 'fact', 'elementary fact', and 'science' as technical terms. The 'world' is composed of 'elementary facts', and is represented by 'sentences' which have 'sense', and which belong to 'science'; but the ethical is not factual, and cannot be so described.

Elsewhere Wittgenstein says that 'theories', 'descriptions', and 'explanations' cannot capture the ethical.

Wittgenstein's, however, is a moderate mysticism. When Hugo von Hofmannsthal cries that words 'leave me in the lurch' or 'crumbled in my mouth like mouldy mushrooms' (von Hofmannsthal, 1984), or when the Taoist says that words attach only to the secondary reality of the 'myriad creatures', they express a thesis of general ineffability—the view that language is *altogether* inadequate. In opposition, Naïve Representationalism amounts to the thesis of the general efficacy of language in describing everything without distinction. These two polar views—that everything is mystical, and that nothing is mystical—run counter to common experience, and part of the achievement of the *Tractatus* is that it incorporates the mystical, the representational, and the syntactic into a single, broader, perspective.

For Wittgenstein, the world may be all that is the case, but it is not all that is. The domain of facts is all that representational language can describe, but the syntactic and the mystical have their own reality. In contrast to the reductive, homogenising, 'nothing-but' effect of Naïve Representationalism, the representational, the syntactic and the mystical are all allowed to live.

It has often been suggested that the remarks on the mystical are out of place in the *Tractatus*. But while it is true that it is unusual to find a discussion of the ineffable in a book much of which concerns logic, this only emphasises the contribution of the work to the theory of representation. For the *Tractatus* shows that the great mirror's three sides are not incommensurable, and can be viewed and considered together.

The diversity of the *Tractatus* is obvious in its investigation of a variety of topics—but if this were its whole character, the book would be merely interestingly wide-ranging. The unity of the *Tractatus* is also perceptible, although harder to identify—but if this obliterated diversity, as in Naïve Representationalism, the book would be merely hygienically consistent. As it is, the *Tractatus* creates a balanced *Gestalt*, incorporating unity of perspective with diversity of topic, and allowing place—as any mature philosophy of language must—to all three sides of the mirror.

The rest of the present chapter is intended to make two points: first that, outwith the particular context of the Tractarian system,

Wittgenstein's views on the mystical are by no means eccentric or whimsical; and second that, within the context of the Tractarian system, we are not given a satisfactory criterion of demarcation for the mystical domain.

The Mystical in Religion and the Arts

For Wittgenstein, 'the ethical' is the whole realm of value—moral, aesthetic, religious etc. It is perhaps not often claimed that moral matters are indescribable, but in religion and the fine arts it is widely held, especially among practitioners, that what is most important eludes verbal description.

In *The Varieties of Religious Experience*, William James endeavoured to find the common factors in religious or spiritual experience, and the four he identified were (1) ineffability, (2) noetic quality, (3) transiency, and (4) passivity (James, 1952). It is frequently stated in this context that what is most essential lies '... far hidden from the reach of words' (Wordsworth, 'The Prelude', Book III). Lao Tzu's *Tao Te Ching*, for example, opens with the lines:

> The *Tao* that can be spoken of,
> Is not the eternal *Tao*.

The doctrine of ineffability is prominent in many spiritual traditions, especially in Japanese Zen Buddhism, and in the Chinese Ch'an Buddhism from which it derived. Bodhidharma, the First Patriarch of the Ch'an school, referred to the method as 'A special transmission outside the scriptures; no dependence on words or letters ...' (Humphreys, 1976, p32). In the Zen tradition, among others, language is linked to the discursive intellect, and it is the inability of the intellect to capture what is spiritual, rather than a limitation specific to language, which is emphasised. In particular, it is held, language and the intellect operate with distinctions and oppositions, and in the state of mind which is sought—*Satori*—these are dissolved.

In the arts also, what is most valuable—aesthetic experience—eludes verbal description. If I go to a concert, a performance of dance, or an exhibition of paintings, I cannot then give someone else an adequate description of my reaction. The concert, the dance, or the painting does not have a content which can be expressed in any of various media, including the medium of verbal description—and if it did, it would be enough to read about it. It is possible to make technical points concerning interpretation and execution, and it is possible in this vein to make historical and comparative points, but one's actual *aesthetic* reaction cannot adequately be conveyed in words. To this end, the most which can be done is to use suggestive metaphors and similies, but if the other person is not acquainted with the work, even this conveys little. This is not to say that the points which can be made are intrinsically wrong, and it is not to say that they are uninteresting or uninformative, but regarding the aesthetic itself, they are largely irrelevant.

This restricts what can effectively be said, for example, in a newspaper review of a concert: the standard of the musicians' execution, the conductor's sense of rhythm, and the more technical aspects of his interpretation can be described and hence criticised, but these are all means to an end, and what is most important can only be gestured at. The performance of a passage can of course be described as 'glorious', 'yearning', 'moving' etc., but the amount conveyed by such terms is very minimal, and reading the review cannot be a substitute for attending the concert. (It is often said that aesthetic reaction is 'subjective': the point here is that it is verbally incommunicable, not that it is idiosyncratic.)

In rehearsals, the interaction between a conductor and an orchestra does contain a verbal element. The conductor will ask the second violins to play a passage more quietly, he will ask the bassoonist to play a sequence of notes in a more *staccato* manner etc. But even when indicating phrasing, he has to use manual or facial gestures, or sing the passage. It is significant in this respect that the expressions in the international vocabulary of Italian terms used in music mostly concern technical points of execution: *piano, allegro, rubato, diminuendo* etc. Some of these terms, such as *animato* and *maestoso* are quasi-aesthetic, but these only give a rough idea of how a passage is to be played, and they only convey to a minimal extent the aesthetic impression to be created by the particular passage in the particular piece being rehearsed. A conductor does not usually stand up at the beginning of a rehearsal and give a prolonged lecture on the aesthetic impression he wants to create, and if he does so, it is unlikely that this will be effective. Rather, as the rehearsal proceeds, and the execution of the piece is altered in various ways, it becomes clearer what is desired. The means to the end can be described and criticised, but the end itself, though it can be perceived, cannot be properly stated. It is significant in this respect that the conductor's profession is one of the few co-operative occupations in which it is unnecessary to be a linguist in order to work effectively in different countries. Apart from the standard terms describing execution, the conductor's most effective means of communication is through the gestures made with his hands or with his baton.

It is true that the conductor and the orchestra work together to produce an aesthetic effect which is usually better than that produced by the first run-through of the piece. And it is true that the conductor and orchestra speak to one another. But the nature of this interaction is not one in which the conductor *says* what *aesthetic* effect he wants, and the orchestra does as he asks—otherwise it would be enough for him to write the orchestra a letter.

The point might be put by saying that the musicians work within the factual world to produce an aesthetic effect which is outwith the factual world. The instruments, the manual movements etc. are factual, and plainly physical, while the aesthetic result is not; and so the means is describable, while the end is ineffable.

It is often said that music and painting 'cannot be taught' or 'cannot be learned from a book'. The point is not that a teacher or a book cannot help the student on technical issues, but rather that the guiding appreciation of the aesthetic impression to be created cannot be transferred by verbal means. And even with respect to what can be communicated, bodily gesture plays an important rôle: it would be easy to tell someone over the telephone how to get from Green Park to Picadilly on the London Underground, but a music lesson conducted in this way would be severely hampered. It is true that a book can help a student on technical points, but it is not true that an adequate description of what is essential and aesthetic is given *in* the book, and is transferred to the student when he reads it. Even at the level of manual execution, it is often difficult for the teacher to tell the student in literal language what he or she should do, and it is frequently more effective to use analogy and metaphor, saying that the kinaesthetic feeling of executing some particular technique is *like* that of some other well known action. In teaching violin bow technique, for example, reference is made to such sensations as those of catching a bouncing ball, and applying thick paint.

In the field of human relations also, it seems that much of what is essential eludes description. If two people are friends, for example, they can certainly describe the external, circumstantial, and behavioural factors in their relationship, and they can describe one another's characters and attitudes; but the essential nature of the relationship is difficult or impossible to express, and has to be indicated *through* description of these other factors. If one person describes to another a friendship which he or she has, the albeit important points which are made lie, so to speak, to the side of the actual topic of discussion. The listener may then try to imagine himself or herself in this situation—in the speaker's place—and may divine how the speaker feels, but this is not the same as straightforwardly being told a fact.

Statements by artists and theorists alike, to the effect that art cannot be 'understood' or 'explained' and addresses something not captured by words, are myriad:

> Everyone wants to understand art. Why not try to understand the song of a bird? People who try to explain pictures are usually barking up the wrong tree. [Pablo Picasso, quoted in Goldwater and Treves, 1976, p421]

> One could not express in words what one feels with one's eyes and one's hand. [Alberto Giacometti, quoted in Ashton, 1985, p57]

> A painter should always imagine he is painting for someone with no gift of articulate speech. [Paul Valéry, 1960, vol. 12, p87]

> The necessity for the plastic symbols of the art of painting is to some extent dictated by the inadequacy of our linguistic means of communication. To explain art, therefore, is often an effort to give words to nameless processes ... [Herbert Read, 'Introduction', in Klee, 1948, p v]

In religion and the arts at least, it is a commonplace that what is essential eludes verbal description, and that the most that can be done is to talk *around* it, or to address the practical means by which it is produced.

This is not to say that Wittgenstein's treatment is complete: it is very brief, and does not address the questions which immediately arise concerning the rôle of shared experience in communication, subjectivity and relativity of value, the relations between language, understanding, explanation, and feeling etc.

And it is not to say that Wittgenstein's view is original: as argued above, it expresses common experience, and many thinkers who may have influenced him asserted the existence of the ineffable.[1]

Rather, the value of Wittgenstein's treatment of the mystical consists in its lack of originality—the well grounded belief in the ineffable is incorporated into the Tractarian perspective, thus creating a breadth of vision, and a non-triviality, uncommon in the philosophy of language. To complain that the remarks on the mystical are not original, or that they are out of place, is to miss this point. The *Tractatus* gives us no new thoughts *about* the ineffable: what it does is to encompass the mystical in its scheme, so allowing us to cast one glance over all three sides of the great mirror of language. And this is surely right: the ineffable is here to stay, and it is therefore the task of the philosophy of language to accommodate it, rather than to dismiss it.

Within the context of the Tractarian system and the Tractarian terminology, Wittgenstein's points about ineffability somehow seem abstruse and contentious. However, despite this appearance, they are—at least in the spiritual and aesthetic realms—the expression of common experience. In those areas of life which involve ineffability, the limits of language may not often be discussed and stated, but they are certainly understood and assumed. And so it seems that the points in the *Tractatus* which are most widely held outside the philosophical community are those made near the end of the book. What is perhaps most striking is that ineffability is not only real, but unproblematic: in the relevant activities we get on very well without words.

The Demarcation of the Mystical

It cannot be said, though, that Wittgenstein's discussion is itself unproblematic. In particular, it is not clear that the line between what can and what cannot be described is as sharp as Wittgenstein's discussion suggests, or that it falls exactly where he says it does. On one hand, we have no guarantee that language has the potential to give a wholly adequate representation of everything factual. And on

---

[1]For a discussion of possible influences on this aspect of Wittgenstein's thought, see Janik and Toulmin, 1973, chapters 4 and 5.

the other hand, the religious and the aesthetic do seem to admit of a minimal degree of description through metaphor and poetry.

It might be argued, in favour of a sharp division between the mystical and the describable, that metaphorical and poetical discourse can be clearly distinguished from normal, literal discourse, and does not constitute proper description. But metaphor is a matter of degree, and there is a continuum passing from literal speech, through 'dead' metaphor, to 'live' metaphor. Ordinary discourse contains a multitude of half-dead metaphors, and these words owe some of their semantic resonance to their original non-metaphorical meanings, as is brought out if there is 'mixing'. For example, the awkwardness of the phrases 'he devoured the new perspective' and 'this is the highest of fundamentals' is due to the practical impossibilities of eating something visual and of being both high and low. Thus literal discourse differs in degree rather than in kind from metaphorical discourse, and we cannot neatly divide them from one another.

Wittgenstein makes it quite clear that the mystical does not belong to the 'world' of 'facts', and that its study cannot be a 'science', but he does give more attention to removing it from the world than to locating it exactly outside the world. It is not suggested, though, that these things constitute internal syntactic features of representational systems, and it is certainly not a doctrine of the *Tractatus* that they are to be grouped together with logical relations, probability, modality etc. It is evident that Wittgenstein means in these passages to address something beyond the reach of language, rather than something internal to it: something behind, rather than inside, the great mirror.

Wittgenstein's strategy in delineating the mystical is not to address it directly. His intention is rather to give an explicit description of what is *not* mystical, and so by the same act to draw a boundary on the other side of which lies what *is* mystical. A line has two sides, and the idea is to say what is on one side, and where it ends, and thus by implication indicate the what is on the other side, without the error of directly talking about it. In the *Tractatus* he says of philosophy:

> It will signify what cannot be said, by presenting clearly what can be said. [T 4.115]

And discussing the *Tractatus* in a letter to Ludwig von Ficker, he wrote:

The book's point is an ethical one ... My book draws limits to the
sphere of the ethical from the inside as it were, and I am convinced
that this is the ONLY rigorous way of drawing those limits. [Janik
and Toulmin, 1973, p192]

The project is to delimit the ethical from inside the *factual*—
from what is not ethical. Paul Englemann discussed theses issues at
length with Wittgenstein, and later wrote:

When he nevertheless takes immense pains to delimit the unimportant, it is not the coastline of the island which he is bent on
surveying with such meticulous accuracy, but the boundary of the
ocean. [Englemann, 1967, p97]

The idea is that a delineation of the 'unimportant' factual world
would also serve as a delineation of the mystical.

What is perhaps most surprising is that Wittgenstein does not
in this context exploit the *atomistic* character of his account of representation. It is often suggested that the ineffable has a holistic,
Gestalt, or even undifferentiated nature which cannot be captured
in language. The thought is that this organic wholeness does not reduce without remainder when dismantled in atomistic analysis, and
that language is inevitably atomistic, analytical, contrastive, or differential. Wittgenstein's account of representational language, and
of the world it describes, is thoroughly atomistic, and so he is in
a position to use and investigate atomicity as a criterion by which
to differentiate the factual world from the mystical. Oddly enough,
though, he does not do so.

In any case, two problems attend Wittgenstein's undeclared strategy. The first is simply that outside the factual world lie not only
the mystical, but also the syntactic, and so to show that something
is non-factual is not enough.

The second, less soluble, problem is that with this strategy, the
shortcomings of the Tractarian account of the factual transfer to that
of the mystical. In particular, we lack a method of analysis, and so
we cannot, on the basis of what is provided in the *Tractatus*, actually
draw the delimiting line. If we had to discover whether something
were factual or ethical, we should have to determine whether it were
a *Sachverhalt* (or a *Tatsache*) or not: but since we cannot identify
configurations of Tractarian objects, we cannot do this. And on the

linguistic side, since it is not explained how to reduce an ordinary sentence to a truth-function of *Elementarsätze*, we cannot tell in individual cases whether sentences are fact-stating or not. Thus the problem of the absence of a method of analysis, which vitiates the Tractarian theory of representational language, arises again with respect to the mystical.

Part V

CONCLUSION

Chapter 10

Summary

Overview

We have now followed Wittgenstein through the *Tractatus*, surveying all three sides of the 'great mirror' of language.

Reflected in the mirror we find an atomistic world of elementary facts, which are independent of one another, and which are composed of elementary unanalysable objects. Ordinary language does not directly represent this world, but decomposes into elementary sentences which depict elementary facts through the pairing of names with objects, and the matching of structures.

Inside the mirror we find 'syntactic' features and relations internal to the representational system of language. These may seem to belong to the world, rather than to the mirror itself, and much argument in the *Tractatus* is devoted to opposing this tendency. As a result, they are placed not in the factual world, nor in what is essentially its analogue—the platonic world of special platonic facts, but inside language itself. In establishing the intra-syntactic reality, and the independence from the world, of these inner features of language, the *Tractatus* does for linguistic representation what abstract art has done for visual representation. The syntactic has a life of its own, it 'takes care of itself', it says nothing about the world and nature, it does not depend on them, and it should be investigated as such. However, unreliant on the world, it is nevertheless part of the apparatus of representation in which the world is reflected. Logic, probability, possibility, necessity, identity, the objects of mathematics and scientific theory, and the causes of philosophical error are all

165

assigned to the syntactic category. Logic receives the most extended examination, and this weaves a compounded web, which involves the *Grundgedanke*, the Logical Independence Thesis, and the theory of truth-functions, and which leads to a deprecatory account of the complexities of logical inference, and an investigation of the alternative possibility of a perspicuous notation.

Behind the mirror we find the mystical realm of value, which cannot be represented in language. What Wittgenstein says actually expresses a consensus view among those who work in the relevant fields, and poses a standing challenge to Naïve Representationalist philosophy of language. However, the Tractarian strategy for demarcating the mystical is itself unworkable.

Within the Tractarian conceptual scheme, the distribution of the various topics investigated, and of the technical terms used, can be sketched out as below. The diagram is intended as a sketch, and there are certainly details of the *Tractatus* which it does not portray. Tautologies and contradictions, for example, are 'degenerate' cases of truth-functional sentences: they are of the same type as representational sentences, but they do not themselves represent anything in the world. Some inhabitants of the world of facts—objects, and formal properties of facts—cannot be described, and so have something in common with the occupants of the mystical division. And 'nonsense' characterises incoherent and, more importantly, *psuedo-representational* statements—those which speak about something mystical or syntactic as if it were a representable fact.

REPRESENTATIONAL LANGUAGE	NON-REPRESENTATIONAL LANGUAGE	NONSENSICAL LANGUAGE
'natural science', 'saying', 'sense', 'sentences', 'doctrines', 'hypotheses' etc.	'senselessness', 'saying nothing'	'pseudo sentences' (psuedo-representational statements)
logically molecular sentences		
logically atomic sentences		
elementary sentences		
names, configurations		

THE WORLD	THE SYNTACTIC	THE MYSTICAL
facts	logic, probability, modality, identity,	the ethical, the aesthetic, the religious, etc.
elementary facts		
objects, configurations	objects of mathematics and scientific theory, causes of philosophical error	

External Influences

It is certain that various influences in Wittgenstein's Viennese cultural background bore on his early thought. The *Tractatus* addresses the theory of representation, and the critique of representation was very much in the air in various forms in *fin-de-siècle* Vienna. The Tractarian account of representational language owes much to the views of Hertz, Boltzmann, and Mach. The Tractarian treatment of the syntactic in representation is akin to the Kantian treatment of the 'categories' in knowledge, transformed into its linguistic analogue. The notion that language can mislead us, in particular through the positing of falsely reified entities, is reminiscent of the *Sprachkritik* of Krauss and Mauthner. And the Tractarian views on the mystical resonate with those of Kierkegaard, Schopenhauer, Tolstoy, Haecker, and von Hofmannsthal. As a result, when Wittgenstein discovered the logic and philosophy of language of Russell and Frege, it is clear that he approached these from his own independent standpoint, with his own pre-existing preoccupations, and used them for his own purposes.

These external influences were vitally important in the formation of Wittgenstein's early thought (see especially Janik and Toulmin, 1967). However the *result* of these forces was a synthesis rather than an aggregate, 'no mixture but a structure' (cf LO p24), an organic unity with a life of its own. The Tractarian perspective which emerged from these origins was a balanced *Gestalt*, and was genuinely new. And the objective of the present exposition has accordingly been the internal one of approaching the contents of the *Tractatus* from the standpoint of its *own* perspective and associated conceptual scheme.

The Tractarian Perspective

The *Tractatus* evidently incorporates both unity and diversity. The book's diversity is immediately seen in the variety of themes investigated, but its unity is initially only *sensed*, and one feels driven to discover its origin. What is crucial is that the unity of the *Tractatus* derives from a perspective rather than a proposition—from a schema rather than a doctrine. Throughout the book, Wittgenstein is concerned to address the great mirror of language from *all three sides*, and accordingly his persistent opposition is to the Naïve Representationalist, who would allow the mirror only one side. It is this, rather than any explicit or implicit doctrine which gives the book its coherence, and which most determines its character. The *Tractatus* does not constitute a single deductive argument—rather it constitutes the investigation of a range of topics from a common three-sided perspective.

It could be argued of course that what I have called a 'perspective' might equally be seen as a set of propositions, to the effect that language has a representational function, internal features, and limits. This would however be rather vacuous, since such propositions do not play the rôle of axioms within the *Tractatus*. The actual arguments of the *Tractatus* concern much more specific and detailed points, and do not *follow from* these more general thoughts. Rather, these thoughts provide a matrix through which the specific arguments of the *Tractatus* are put to work. Influence is mutual here, though, since the development of the various individual arguments enriches and confirms the value of the original perspective.

The influence of the Tractarian perspective has a number of consequences for the way Wittgenstein proceeds, and for the way he should be interpreted.

First, there is nothing random about the ideas which Wittgenstein attacks. The relevance of the views he opposes is determined by his general perspective, and in particular he attacks views which would assign something to the wrong side of the mirror, or which would render it one-sided altogether. Wittgenstein's responses carry their own perspective, they need to be assessed in their own terms, and it would be wrong, for example, to equate his world-view with that of a British empiricist.

Second, the point of many of the arguments in the *Tractatus* is to move something from one side of the mirror to another. It is argued that a logical constant is not just one more object-denoting name; that a statement about logic or scientific principles is not just one more representational, world-oriented factual statement; that probability is not just another relation to be found in the world; that identity is not another relation between objects; that the objects of philosophical investigation are not factual; that ethical or aesthetic value is not another attribute among those which attach wordly facts and objects etc. The general effect of the *Tractatus* is to spread things out, and what it opposes is the collapsing of everything into the categories of the factual and fact-stating discourse. This differential tendency, within the categories of the general scheme, creates some of the character of the *Tractatus*. And one suspects that the hidden enemy, Naïve Representationalism, often has as its silent ally the Fallacy of Grammatical Analogy: the credibility of the views Wittgenstein attacks derives from our speaking about the syntactic and the mystical much as we speak about the factual.

Third, although it is natural to look for the origin of the unity of the *Tractatus*, the attempt to root the Tractarian *Gestalt* in a single doctrine does violence to the work. Whether this is the picture theory, the *Grundgedanke*, or the *N* operator, and whether it is held to be explicit or implicit, the result is a curious intellectual tension, and, symptomatically, a radical re-structuring of the book.

Fourth, there is a degree of independence between the *details* of the *Tractatus* and its perspective. There are certainly imperfect details in the *Tractatus*: the picture theory of meaning's vulnerable internal relation of depiction, the middle passages' reticence on the exact nature of the syntactic, the unworkable strategy in demarcating the mystical, the obscurity of presentation, the odd terminology etc. But the Tractarian *Gestalt* is an emergent property, and can survive some deficiencies in its components.

Fifth, since it not a pivot but a matrix which holds the *Tractatus* together, there is considerable independence between its specific doctrines and arguments. In particular, the middle sections on the inside of the mirror, and the final remarks on the mystical are independent of the early treatment of representation. What is said about the syntactic and the mystical does not rely on the particulars of the paraphernalia of depiction—analysis, elementary sentences, configurations of objects, pictorial form etc.

This last point bears especially on what we take to be the legacy of the *Tractatus*. For if we take the book to be based on the picture theory of meaning, then its legacy is merely the investigation of a mistake. But what is of primary importance in the *Tractatus* is its own perspective, with the resulting conceptual scheme, and breadth of vision, in the theory of representation. As a result, the most valuable philosophical legacy of the *Tractatus* is not its particular doctrines, correct or incorrect, but the perspective by which it is informed—the three-sided mirror.

Epilogue I

The Tractatus and Cognitive Science

The Computer Model of the Mind

Cognitive science is essentially the clustering of workers from a number of different fields around the computer model of the mind. The 'component disciplines' from which these workers come are principally artificial intelligence, philosophy, psychology, linguistics and neuroscience, and what gives coherence to the presently heterogeneous new discipline is the belief that cognition can be modelled in a manner given by, or inspired by, the computer.

This general view has myriad attractions: in psychology it allows theories to be investigated through the building of working models on a computer, it seems to offer a release from both the explanational strictures of behaviourism and the mystification of mentalism, in philosophy it is associated with functionalism which purports to solve the mind-body problem, and in general it broadens the significance of the computer and increases the tractability of some of the elusive objects of the component disciplines of cognitive science (see Gardner, 1985).

The 'computer model of the mind' can mean many things—and the computer program can be asked to serve as anything from a useful tool to an isomorphic replica of thought. However one thesis—inspired by the computer, though not inseparable from it—has come close to constituting a paradigm during the first phase of life of the 'mind's new science'. This is the thesis of 'classical cognitivism', that cognition essentially involves a symbol processing system, or physical

171

symbol system (Newell and Simon, 1976). *Cognition and intelligence consist in portraying the world through a symbolic medium of syntactically structured mental representation—a language of thought—and in manipulating that medium.* Classical cognitivism has recently come under increasingly critical scrutiny, especially from the PDP or connectionist school (see Clark, 1989; and Smolensky, 1988), and there is a growing need for 'a completely general theory of representation' (Dennett, 1981, p91). The subject of Wittgenstein's *Tractatus* is the theory of representation, and the purpose of the present epilogue is to give brief attention to two points at which this work of 1921 is relevant to the current debate. The classical cognitivist view divides cognition into representational data, and syntactic manipulation of that data, and the relations of the *Tractatus* to these two issues will be discussed in turn.

The Picture Theory in Cognitive Science

One champion of classical cognitivism, and the concept of mental representation, is Jerry Fodor. According to Fodor, we have a 'language of thought'—an internal code in which we represent the world. This code is innate, symbolic, and analogous to a computer's machine code. It has the expressive power of natural language, and statements in natural language are compiled down to it (Fodor, 1975). The basic idea goes as far back as William of Ockham (see Geach, 1957, §23), and has great appeal, for example, in cognitive psychology where it helps to explain the interaction of diverse cognitive processes, through positing a common medium of cognition.

We are asked to believe that natural language reduces to an elementary code, and that this, without further help, represents the world. What is immediately striking is the similarity with Wittgenstein's picture theory of meaning, and it has been argued by John Heil (1981) that Fodor's language of thought is inadmissible, essentially because it has the same vices as Wittgenstein's picture theory.

The two postulated elementary languages—Fodor's language of thought, and Wittgenstein's elementary sentences—also have the same primary virtue: semantic autonomy. In both cases the language 'takes care of itself', and represents reality 'off its own bat' (N, pp43, 26): meaning has been *naturalised*, and a semantic terminus is provided at which contact is made with reality without further help and without further ado. Indeed, if we regard the language of thought as hard-wired into the brain, then we have essentially a picture-theory of brain-states, explaining cognitive 'projection', or 'aboutness' in general (through isomorphism between brain-states and represented facts).

What Heil argues is that in order to work, Fodor's theory must adopt various details of Wittgenstein's—and so in becoming plausible, it becomes implausible. In particular, says Heil, Fodor needs to assume an *internal* relation between his elementary representations and the facts they represent, for otherwise the theory loses its main strength (and becomes reliant, for example, on the postulation of inner *homunculi* which determine meaning—this being a re-statement of the problem).

The best candidate for this internal relation is Tractarian *structural isomorphism*—the matching of natural structure between elementary sentence and fact depicted—and here Heil objects on two counts. First, structure—and hence also structural isomorphism—is relative: *things and situations do not have one natural structure*, and structural equivalence can be discovered 'with a little ingenuity, for *any* two complexes' (Heil, 1981, p339).[1] Second, the view implies that *every* case of structural equivalence is a case of representation, and this seems unlikely, especially given the relativity of structural isomorphism.

It might be added that isomorphism is a symmetrical relation, whereas representation is not: we talk *about* the world, and represent it, but it does not talk about us, nor represent us.

Fodor's case is that much theory in cognitive science is committed, albeit tacitly, to his thesis of a language of thought. And Heil's case is that Fodor is in turn committed to something like the Tractarian picture theory. Thus, the problems of the picture theory reappear as the—initially invisible—difficulties of a naïve theory of mental representation in cognitive science. The point is not of course that cognitive science *must* commit itself to such a theory of representation, but rather that if it does, then its difficulties turn out to be of a surprisingly Tractarian sort.

An alternative Wittgensteinian attack on a naïve picture theory of mental representation is provided by William Shebar (reported

---

[1]The issue of the relativity of structure to purpose is also discussed in T.C. Potts, 1977.

in Gardner, 1985, pp336-8). Rather than appealing to the faults
of the *Tractatus*, Shebar appeals to one of its most fruitful ideas—
the Fallacy of Grammatical Analogy. The argument is, essentially,
that the very idea of a medium of *internal* representation is suspect, and is based on a mistaken analogy with the usual conception
of outer symbols and representations. When speaking about mental
images, we speak in such a way as to reify them—we make them into
things—and we speak as if we had a private mental 'slide show' in
which 'hidden pictures' were shown. The case is similar to one given
by Wittgenstein (at *Zettel*, §69)—the surface grammar of imagining something is like that of eating something, buying something
etc.; but while the latter cases imply the existence of an *object*, the
former does not (see chapter 8). The notion of imagining an inner
picture, Shebar argues, is no more than an extended metaphor, and
it is misleading to the extent that in this context '... the problems
of psychology will be solved not by newer data or more precise terminology, but, rather, by the realisation that they are not genuine
problems' (Gardner, *op cit*, p337).

Syntactic Manipulation

A physical symbol system does not just store data—it performs syntactic symbol-crunching on that data as well. It is natural to ask
what purpose this processing serves, and in particular whether it
generates *new knowledge* or just *new representations of old knowledge*.

Let us take the case where the processing is done by an inter-
preter for the programming language Prolog, and the medium of
representation is the predicate calculus (see Kowalski, 1979).

A Prolog program is composed of 'facts' (literals) and 'rules'
(implicative statements), represented in the Horn-clause variant of
the predicate calculus. When the program is given to a computer
the result is an act of syntax-crunching which performs the logical
deduction of a conclusion from the set of premises in the program.
What the program has discovered for us is that the logical relation
of entailment holds between the premises and the conclusion (and a
trace of the execution of the program together with the resolution-
rule of inference would constitute a formal proof of this relation).

From a Tractarian perspective, we are of course dealing with the inside of the mirror: the 'discovery' of a logical relation tells us nothing new about the factual world, but merely reveals a connection between sentences (see chapter 6). It might be proposed that what the execution of a Prolog program discovers, assuming the truth of the premises in the program, is the truth of the conclusion derived (which is a factual statement). However nothing *new* has been discovered about the world, since the sense of the conclusion was already contained in that of the (conjoined) premises originally entered into the computer, albeit using different syntax (cf T 5.122).

However, the execution of the program evidently tells us *something*, for otherwise, having written it, we should have no need to execute it. It is sometimes said that the conclusion deduced by the program is 'implicit' in the premises. However this does not solve the problem, rather it states it: the premises have already stated what the conclusion states, but we do not know this without mechanical help.

Here, the *Tractatus* provides the insight that the notation we use is non-perspicuous to the degree that, in complex cases, we need mechanical aid to discover the intra-syntactic relations between sentences (see chapter 7; and cf T 6.1262). The sense of the conjoined premises does contain the sense of the conclusion (in this case the Prolog 'query'), and this is a matter of the syntactic structures of the sentences themselves, but our notation is such as to obscure this. The Prolog execution does tell us something: it tells us something about syntax. And the odd epistemological consequence is that this is necessary only when we do not fully know what we mean.

The situation is illustrated by the case of two logically equivalent programs only the second of which explicitly contains the conclusion in question. The sense of the conclusion is contained in the senses of both programs, and indeed both programs have the same sense, but this is obscured by our notation. In the simplest case we can derive a conclusion from a program, and then add it as a 'lemma' to the original program to form a second program. In the second program the entailment of the conclusion is syntactically obvious, and is easier for the computer to discover, though the second program has the same sense as the first, and the difference is merely notational.

I do not mean to suggest that this is an end to the matter: in particular, when we move to inference which is not pure logical deduction, the case is less obvious. However, it does seem that in the present context the *Tractatus* has a direct bearing on cognitive science: even if we do maintain that cognition consists in the manipulation of an inner language of thought, we cannot maintain that this manipulation is purely deductive, for cognition surely consists in more than just assisting ourselves with non-perspicuous syntax.

Epilogue II

The Tractatus and Abstract Art

Introduction

Wittgenstein's early philosophy was developed during the second decade of the 20th century—he went to Cambridge in 1911, and the *Tractatus* was published in 1921. During this same period, the abstractionist movement in art sprang up in several places in Europe. What is remarkable is the kindredness between the two: what the abstract art movement did for visual representation, the *Tractatus* did for linguistic representation.

The present epilogue is intended briefly to address this specific point in the theory of representation. It is not directed at those questions in the history of ideas concerning influences, movements, and *Zeitgeister*, nor at questions of sociological cause, nor at the issue of whether plastic art is inherently linguistic.

Non-Representation

Abstraction in plastic art was not, of course, new, as was argued at the time by Wilhelm Worringer in his *Abstraktion und Einfühlung* of 1908. However, the sudden and widespread development of abstraction in this critical decade was unprecedented. The development went under many names, and occurred in many places. In Munich there were Wassily Kandinsky and Franz Marc, and their group *Der Blaue Reiter* which was formed in 1911. In Amsterdam there was

Piet Mondrian and *De Stijl*, in Moscow there was suprematism, and
so on.

What is characteristic of abstract art is the renunciation of representation of the world. As Kandinsky put it in 1912:

> The 'representational' reduced to a minimum must in abstraction
> be regarded as the most intensely effective reality. [Kandinsky,
> 1974, p165]

Instead of depicting subjects from life or nature, the abstract qualities of *form, line, colour, and surface* are investigated for their own sake. Figurative, representational, imitative, realist, or naturalistic art had been 'enslaved' to nature. What was sought was an emancipation from imitative depiction of the world, and the consequent freedom to exploit the patterns and interactions of pure forms and colours on the canvas.

Kandinsky was the first practising artist to write an extended account of the principles of abstract art—in his *Über das Geistige in der Kunst* of 1912. Here he speaks of the 'mutual influence of form and colour' (Kandinsky, 1977, p29) and 'the various forms which, by standing in different relationships to each other, decide the composition of the whole' (*op cit*, p39)

His concern is not with depiction of the world, but with the autonomous harmonies and inner relations between colours and forms—the patterns, balances, repetitions and rhythms within the painting. Rather than telling a story from life, the abstract painting exploits the inner characteristics of pure colour and form.

Kandinsky had a strong sense of cultural evolution, and speaks of the necessarily gradual development of abstraction through 'the rejection of the third dimension' (*op cit*, p44), and through the presentation of non-natural combinations of form and colour—a red horse, or for that matter a blue rider (*op cit*, p49). In relinquishing projective depth (perspective, figurative shadow etc.), and in combining abstract elements in ways not found in nature, the autonomy of form and colour are emphasised and discovered.

Kandinsky also extends his discussion of these internal relations to the transaesthetic interactions and relations of the different senses, linking colour and form together with sound, smell, taste, temperature, texture and movement (kinaesthesia). He speaks of colours which are warm or cold, which approach or retreat—yellow approaches, blue retreats, and green is static—sharp colours and sharp forms, yellow sounds, the movement of a triangle etc. His leading metaphors are musical—the 'rhythms' and 'harmonies' of forms and colours—this being the paradigmatically non-representational art (*op cit*, p19).

A similar development took place in literature, for example in the work of Gertrude Stein—written under the influence of cubism. Here, language is used in a reflexive, non-projective way, descriptive content is reduced, and new intra-textual forms and patterns are investigated through such techniques as varying rhythmic repetition (see, for example, her *Tender Buttons* of 1914).

Internal Relations

What is striking—and this is the main point of the present epilogue—is that these are *internal relations*: they have nothing to do with the world, and subsist entirely *within* the painting, at least as perceived by the human eye. The harmonies, relationships, and 'counterpoints' which are set up are *internal* to the *Gestalt* of the painting. The renunciation of projection onto the world allows attention to shift to the inner features and relations of visual representation.

In the *Tractatus* it is argued, in effect, that philosophy and scientific theory are non-figurative—they investigate the representational medium itself, rather than putting it to its normal imitative use. The discipline of Logic is non-realist—it concerns something present *in* our linguistic representations, not something depicted by them. Probability, modality, and identity are non-natural, and so on.

And in abstract art, the qualities of form, line, colour, and surface are recognised as having a life of their own, independent of the representation of facts. They 'take care of themselves' (cf T 5.473; N pp1,11,43), we do not have to 'look at the world' in order to investigate them (cf T 5.551), and in a painting they are 'shown' or exhibited, rather than 'said'. The representational content of a painting, in contrast, comes nearer to being a propositional statement which is justified by the world it depicts (cf T 6.113, 2.224).

Thus abstractionism in art does for visual representation what the *Tractatus* does for linguistic representation—each affirms the reality and autonomy of the internal relations of its representational medium.

And in both cases what is opposed is Naïve Representationalism. In the linguistic case, this is the assignation of logic and other things syntactic to the world of facts, as quietly urged on us by the Fallacy of Grammatical Analogy. And in the visual case, it is the recognition of that medium only as a vehicle for factual representation of the world, nature and life.

Abstraction and Figuration in Philosophy and Art

In characterising abstract art, it is not enough just to say that nature is renounced, form is set free, and the subject is obliterated. It must also be asked what 'abstraction' is, and what relation it bears, or should bear, to representation.

It has been argued that visual art should divorce itself totally from representation, and that formal, abstract features are the *only* aesthetically valuable elements in a painting (see Bell, 1914; Fry, 1920). Few artists, however, have followed this to its extreme. Picasso, for example, never wholly renounced representation, and Kandinsky says of the total abandonment of representation:

> Must we then abandon utterly all material objects and paint solely in abstractions? ... To deprive oneself of this possibility is to limit one's powers of expression. [*op cit*, p32].

Mondrian, writing in 1936, spoke of the 'dynamic rhythm of determinate mutual relations' which is 'veiled' in figurative art (Mondrian, 1986, p295). Concerning the natural, represented subject of a painting, he wrote:

> For pure art, then, the subject can never be an additional value; it is the line, the colours and their relations which must "bring into play the whole sensual and intellectual register of the inner life" ... not the subject. [*op cit*, p296]

However, Mondrian strongly affirms the 'inseparable unity' of form and content, arguing that the dichotomy between the figurative and the non-figurative is ultimately a false one (*op cit*, p292). Thus he says:

Abstract art is therefore opposed to a natural representation of things, But it is *not opposed to nature* as is generally thought. [*op cit*, p293]

The *Tractatus* provides a valuable perspective on this issue, for in its treatment of the theory of representation, it divides the representational use of the linguistic medium from its inner features—but it also unites them. The representational and syntactic aspects of the linguistic medium are *two aspects of the same thing*. The syntactic is independent of the world, but at the same time it is connected to the world, since it constitutes part of a representational medium. And abstraction in art can be seen as analogous—when art turns to the non-figurative, it looks not away from the mirror, but inside it.

One is reminded here of the Tractarian philosophy of science: a system of mechanics, for example, tells us no facts, but lets us *describe* facts differently. Likewise, an abstract painting tells us no facts, but it can make us *see* the world differently, by acting on our system of visual representation. This bears on the issue of evaluation in art, as it does in the disciplines which the *Tractatus* holds to be intra-syntactic. There is a great difference between a painting which is pointlessly abstract and one which makes us see differently. And there is a similar difference between intellectual work which is pointlessly intra-syntactic, and that which improves our completeness and ease of description—it must, so to speak, let us see better as well as talk differently.

The Tractarian perspective also clarifies what it is to be 'abstract' in the artistic sense. Those things which are abstract are inner features of a medium we normally use to represent nature. As such they are present all the time in representations of nature, and although the 'suppression of figuration' may liberate them, it does not create them.

In art, this liberation from nature allowed a new freedom of combination, and a resultant playfulness. But the danger was felt that it might degenerate into an art which was at once pedantic and trivial (cf Read, 1964, p50). The manipulation of form and colour could become exclusively intellectual; and, in its renunciation of the world, the new art could become merely decorative.

Here, abstractionism in art provides a useful perspective on the dangers which were felt to accompany the 'linguistic turn' in philosophy, which the *Tractatus* helped to create. A philosophical programme which attempts to say nothing about the world, but confines itself to mere intra-syntactic clarification, is surely open to the accusation of triviality. In its concentration on the syntactic, it naturally turns to logic, but the result this century has on occasion been wantonly scholastic—and the use of the predicate calculus sometimes merely decorative. It cannot, however, be said of the *Tractatus* itself that it bends the lens without letting us see better, for in investigating its various topics, its concern is always with their true place *vis a vis* description of the world.

Conclusion

The connection which the *Tractatus* bears to abstractionism in art is of course invisible at the level of detail at which most of the book is written. But with the identification of its perspective, its own general orientation becomes clear, and this link also emerges.

Abstractionism is not the whole of art, and what is characterised above is not the whole of abstract art—Kandinsky, for example, was concerned in his art with emotion and spirituality, and these do not reduce to something quasi-syntactic. But where the analogy between the programmes of Wittgenstein's early philosophy and the abstract art movement does apply, it provides the possibility of mutual illumination.

Appendix

The Translations of 'Tatsache', 'Sachverhalt', 'Satz', and 'Elementarsatz'

Wittgenstein's technical terms *Tatsache, Sachverhalt, Satz*, and *Elementarsatz* are translated here as 'fact', 'elementary fact', 'sentence', and 'elementary sentence', since these give the fairest rendering of his meaning in English. The reasons for these choices are given below.

Tatsache and *Sachverhalt*

Introduction

In a letter to Russell, Wittgenstein explains his use of *Tatsache*:

> 'What is the difference between Tatsache and Sachverhalt?' Sachverhalt is, what corresponds to an Elementarsatz if it is true. Tatsache is what corresponds to the logical product of elementary sentences when this product is true. [LR, p72, Monte Cassino, 19.8.1919]

And it is also made clear in a remark later in the *Tractatus* that Wittgenstein intends a *Tatsache* to be a compound of *Sachverhalte*:

> Even if the world is infinitely complex so that every fact consists of infinitely many elementary facts ... [T 4.2211]

183

By 'logical product' Wittgenstein means conjunction, but this is not
to say that the *Tatsache* itself is *logically* conjunctive: as the *Grundgedanke* dictates, there are no conjunctive facts. A *Sachverhalt* is
ontologically simple, and a *Tatsache* is a *compound* of these, but this
compound does not incorporate the 'logical object' of conjunction.

The German expression *Sachverhalt* which I have translated as
'elementary fact' has been a source of debate. As Wittgenstein makes
clear (for example in T 2.01 and 2.0272) what he means by this word
is an arrangement or configuration of 'objects'. The central meaning
of the German *Sachverhalt* is that of a 'situation' or 'circumstance',
with the connotation that several factors stand in relationship. The
expression is composed of *Sach* which means a thing or entity, and
the verb *verhalten* whose relevant sense is that things stand to one
another in proportion or relationship. The term is thus suitable,
since it carries the two required connotations of a fact and an arrangement of things; but it could not be said that its usual German
meaning is that of a configuration of Tractarian objects (it actually
tends to be used in legal contexts). Rather, by refining the usual
meaning of the expression, Wittgenstein makes use of it in the *Tractatus* as a technical term: instead of inventing a word, he takes over
a term which is roughly appropriate. We must distinguish therefore between the problem of literal translation and that of conveying
what Wittgenstein meant. Since the German term *Sachverhalt* does
not convey what Wittgenstein meant without the aid of the definition given in the *Tractatus* at 2.01, it seems best in deciding on a
translation to be guided by Wittgenstein's own remarks, rather than
by the usual non-technical meaning of the German term.

Pears and McGuinness translate *Sachverhalt* as 'state of affairs'.
This is an accurate literal translation of the German term, but it
does not convey the technical concept intended in the Tractarian
context.

In Ogden's translation of the *Tractatus* 'atomic fact' is given for
Sachverhalt. In the *ontological* sense this fits Wittgenstein's meaning very well: a *Sachverhalt* is the simplest sort of fact, and cannot
be analysed into simpler facts. However, since Russell's writings
on logical atomism, 'atomic' has tended in philosophical contexts to
be used to denote something which is *logically* simple—something
which contains no logical constants or logical objects, and in this
sense its antonym 'molecular' refers to whatever does contain logi-

cal constants or objects (see for example Russell, 1918–19; and his 'Introduction', T p xiii). Wittgenstein does argue that all facts are logically simple, but this is not a consequence of his definition of *Sachverhalt*, and has to be independently asserted and demonstrated in the *Grundgedanke* and its supporting arguments. To say, in the Tractarian terminology, that a *Sachverhalt* is logically simple is not a definitional truth, since a *Sachverhalt* is defined simply as a configuration of objects, and Wittgenstein argues separately that none of these objects can be logical ones (disjunction, material implication, negation etc.). And further, as is often pointed out, Wittgenstein was not able to give examples of *Sachverhalte*: but if all that were required were that the *Sachverhalt* should be logically simple, then this difficulty would not have arisen. Thus, since 'atomic fact' tends to suggest logical as well as ontological simplicity, it is confusing, and tends to misrepresent Wittgenstein's meaning. The distinction between *Sachverhalt* and *Tatsache* in the *Tractatus* is ontological, not logical, and it would be equally misleading to translate *Tatsache* as 'molecular fact'.

It seems natural, then, to translate *Sachverhalt* as 'elementary fact', it being understood that this is an actual, existent configuration of Tractarian objects, and that *Sachverhalte* combine together to form *Tatsachen*, which are compound facts, and that the distinction between the two is ontological rather than logical.

Stenius' Argument that *Sachverhalte* are Possible Facts

It has however been argued by Erik Stenius that in the *Tractatus* a *Sachverhalt* is not an actual fact but a *possible* one, and discussion of this issue will occupy the rest of the present section.

Stenius argues, initially on the basis of German usage, that for Wittgenstein a *Sachverhalt* is a possible fact, of a Tractarian sort, while a *Tatsache* is an actual one. He takes as examples the true sentence (1) 'The moon is smaller than the earth', and the false sentence (2) 'The earth is smaller then the moon', and says:

> Now I think it is in accord with German usage if we call the de
> scriptive content of a sentence of this kind a *Sachverhalt indepen*
> *dently* of its being a fact or not. According to this terminology
> both (1) and (2) can be regarded as describing *Sachverhalte*. The

difference between them is that the *Sachverhalt* described by (*1*)
is a *bestehender Sachverhalt*—an 'existing' *Sachverhalt*—that is a
Tatsache, whereas (*2*) describes a *nicht bestehender Sachverhalt*—
a 'non-existing' *Sachverhalt*—which is not a *Tatsache*. Thus a
Sachverhalt is something that could *possibly* be the case, a *Tatsache* something that *really* is the case. [*Exposition*, p31]

Two errors emerge already: first, as related in more detail below, whatever a *Sachverhalt* is, it is not the *sense*—the descriptive
content—of a sentence. Second, as is clearly stated at T 4.21 and
in Wittgenstein's letter from *Monte Cassino*, it is an *Elementarsatz*
which describes a *Sachverhalt*, not an ordinary sentence such as (*1*)
or (*2*) above.

Stenius acknowledges that his conclusion is at odds with Wittgenstein's letter to Russell from *Monte Cassino*, and with T 2.034
and 4.2211. He starts by saying 'There is no counterpart in English of
the word *Sachverhalt*' (*op cit*, p29). This is at best an exaggeration:
although translations between languages are seldom or never perfect,
Sachverhalt is generally quite well translated as 'state of affairs'. The
German *Sachverhalt* is not a mystery word which defies translation
into English, and in any case this is not really the issue: the word
is a technical term in the *Tractatus*, and it is *Wittgenstein's* usage
rather than general German usage which we have to discover.

Still on the topic of non-technical, and hence non-Tractarian,
German usage, Stenius introduces his putative distinction between
the meanings of *Sachverhalt* and *Tatsache* with the words 'I think it
is in accordance with at least one way of using the words in question
if we make a distinction of the following kind'. This tentativeness is
appropriate: the two German words are not in general distinguished
in the manner he suggests. It is true that *Tatsache* carries a *heavier*
connotation of actuality, while *Sachverhalt* carries a heavier connotation of an arrangement or state of things, but it is not the case
that these two words *oppose* each other with regard to actuality.

The substance of Stenius' argument really attaches to the observation that in the *Tractatus* such turns of phrase as 'existing *Sachverhalt*' (for example T 2.04, 2.05) and 'the *Sachverhalt* exists' (T 4.25)
appear several times. However this does not, as Stenius imagines,
commit Wittgenstein to an ontology of possible facts. We commonly
use a great range of expressions in this way, for example in asking
whether such-and-such exists or not, without intending to indicate

that the *thing* in question is a possibility. If someone asks 'Does London Bridge still exist?', or mentions 'the totality of existing bridges', he or she does not thereby mean that bridges are *possibilia* which may or may not exist, and the same is true of equivalent phrases in German. Existence, as Kant said, is not a predicate, and to treat it as such is to commit a Fallacy of Grammatical Analogy of the sort Wittgenstein himself identified as a source of philosophical confusion (see chapter 8). Stenius assumes, essentially, that in these passages Wittgenstein uses 'exists' as a predicate like other predicates, and he concludes that Wittgenstein intends *Sachverhalte* to be entities which may or may not have the attribute of existence. But we are under no compulsion to read Wittgenstein in this way, and it is quite natural to interpret his remarks concerning the existence of *Sachverhalte* without inferring that *Sachverhalte* are entities of this sort.

Indeed, had Wittgenstein intended his *Sachverhalte* to be subsistent *possibilia* which may acquire and loose the attribute of existence, moving from possibility into actuality and then reverting to bare possibility again, he would surely have made this plainer— rather than leaving us to deduce it from turns of phrase which by no means decisively indicate such a reading.

It is also significant that Stenius' analysis runs contrary to the *Tractarian* account of modality (see chapter 8). The modalities are explained as syntactic rather than factual: possibility is analysed as an attribute of *sentences*, not of facts, and to reconcile this with Stenius' suggestion would require considerable distortion.

Stenius misconstrues the relationship between the points he makes. He suggests that the existence in the text of the *Tractatus* of remarks concerning the existence of *Sachverhalte* 'must imply' the conclusion that *Sachverhalte* are intended to be *possibilia*. What Stenius' observations really indicate is the converse: *if* the weight of evidence were in favour of the view that *Sachverhalte* are *possibilia*, and especially if Wittgenstein had made it clear that this was what he intended, *then* it might be feasible to read the remarks about the existence of *Sachverhalte* in this way. But Wittgenstein did not state that this was what he intended, and the weight of evidence is on the other side.

There are on the other hand several reasons for thinking that in the *Tractatus* a *Sachverhalt* is an actuality rather than a possibility.

First, in Wittgenstein's letter to Russell (LR, p72) and at T 4.2211, both quoted above, it is made clear that the difference between a *Tatsache* and a *Sachverhalt* is one of compoundedness, not one of modality. Wittgenstein wrote this letter very shortly after the completion of the *Tractatus*, and here he was answering a specific question from Russell: it therefore seems unlikely that he should have misrepresented what he intended in the *Tractatus*.

Second, Wittgenstein writes that:

> Objects are what is unalterable and subsistent; their configuration is what is changing and unstable. [T 2.0271]

A configuration of objects, a *Sachverhalt*, then, is something which can change. This is reasonable if we take a *Sachverhalt* to be an actual configuration of objects, but not if we take it to be a possible one: surely it is actual configurations or actual facts which change, while possibilities remain unaltered.

Third, at T 2.0272 Wittgenstein says: 'The configuration of objects produces the *Sachverhalt*', and here there is no mention of possibility. If a *Sachverhalt* were a possible fact, Wittgenstein should have said that the *possible* configuration of objects produces the *Sachverhalt*.

Fourth, Wittgenstein speaks of 'the possibility of the *Sachverhalt*' (T 2.012), 'possible *Sachverhalte*' (T 2.013), and 'all *possible Sachverhalte*' (*alle* möglichen *Sachverhalte*) (T 2.0124). If a *Sachverhalt* were intended to be a possible fact then the mention of possibility in these passages would be redundant, unless Wittgenstein really intended to incorporate the notion of a possible-possible configuration of objects into his system, which seems unlikely.

A Further Argument that *Sachverhalte* are Possible Facts

The following argument might also be presented in favour of the proposal that Wittgenstein intended his *Sachverhalte* to be possibilities rather than actualities, and it might be thought that it makes explicit a line of thought which might motivate a view such as that of Stenius. It might be supposed that (1) in order that an elementary sentence have *sense* there must exist a corresponding *Sachverhalt* (the assumption might be that to have sense is to depict a *Sachverhalt*, or it might be that the sense of an elementary sentence *is* a *Sachverhalt*). If this supposition is put together with the view advanced above that (*2*) *Sachverhalte* are actualities such that in the case of a true elementary sentence a corresponding *Sachverhalt* exists, while in the case of a false one no corresponding *Sachverhalt* exists, it will follow that (*3*) *false elementary sentences have no sense.* (*1*) and (*2*) between them effectively give the same conditions for having sense as for truth, with the result that no room is left for false but meaningful elementary sentences.

The consequence (*3*) is of course unacceptable, and is plainly inconsistent with what Wittgenstein asserts:

> What a picture represents it represents independently of its truth or falsity, by means of its pictorial form. [T 2.22; cf 4.061]

> What a picture represents is its sense. [T 2.221]

According to Wittgenstein, the sense of a picture is independent of its truth-value, and so a picture with a sense may be either true or false, contrary to (*3*). Thus if we attribute both (*1*) and (*2*) to Wittgenstein we thereby attribute to him an inconsistent and mistaken theory.

If on the other hand we make the reasonable assumption that the theory Wittgenstein intended to advance does not have (*3*) as a consequence, we must relieve him of (*1*) or (*2*). If, in the spirit of the present argument, we attribute (*1*) to Wittgenstein, we may therefore be driven to relieve him of (*2*) in favour of Stenius' view (*4*) that *Sachverhalte* are possibilities. On this view *every* elementary sentence with sense will be matched by a corresponding *Sachverhalt*, this being a possible fact, and those which are true will have an actual fact, perhaps a *Tatsache*, corresponding to them in addition.

In this way we might be led from the assumption (*1*) that in the *Tractatus* in order for an elementary sentence to have sense there must be a matching *Sachverhalt*, to the conclusion (*4*) that Wittgenstein's *Sachverhalte* are possible facts. It will be argued below that, on the contrary, the text of the *Tractatus* does not justify the attribution of (*1*) to Wittgenstein, and further that there is good reason to attribute (*2*) to him, which in turn gives us reason to relieve him of (*1*).

Let us first consider the plausibility of (*1*). It might be thought that for Wittgenstein the sense of an elementary sentence *is* a *Sachverhalt*. The question of the sense of an elementary sentence is not discussed specifically, but the issue of the sense of pictures in general is discussed, and it is made clear that their senses are possibilities of some sort. Sense, as emerges from the passages quoted above, is what is 'represented' (*dargestellt*):

> A picture depicts reality by representing a possibility of existence and non-existence of *Sachverhalte*. [T 2.201]

> A picture represents a possible situation in logical space. [T 2.202]

Here, sense—what is 'represented'—is a possibility, and in the *Tractatus* this is usually a 'situation' or a 'possible situation' (*Sachlage* or *mögliche Sachlage*). It is nowhere asserted that this is a *Sachverhalt*, and it is made clear at T 2.201 that it is not: it is a 'possibility of existence and non-existence of *Sachverhalte*', and this itself could hardly be a configuration of Tractarian objects. (At T 4.2 sense is defined as 'agreement and disagreement with possibilities of existence and non-existence of *Sachverhalte*', and again this itself is clearly not a *Sachverhalt*.)

An alternative supposition is that (*1*) is to be construed as the assertion that for an elementary sentence to have sense is for it to depict a *Sachverhalt*. The term 'depict' (*abbilden*) occurs infrequently in the *Tractatus*, and the present supposition is not asserted in the text: it is stated that pictures can depict 'reality' (for example T 2.17, 2.18) or the 'world' (T 2.19), but not that an elementary sentence's having sense depends on its depicting a *Sachverhalt*. The main problem with this supposition is that it is made clear in the *Tractatus* that depiction maybe either 'correct or incorrect' (T 2.17, 2.18): surely if having sense is dependent on depiction of a *Sachverhalt*, it cannot be left open whether this depiction is correct or incorrect, for then any *Sachverhalt* would do and the supposition would loose its force.

What *is* stated in the *Tractatus* is that pictures depict *reality* (for example T 2.17, 2.171, 2.18, 2.201), 'reality' being 'the existence and non-existence of *Sachverhalte*' (T 2.06). And it might very reasonably be suggested that to be a picture, to have sense, and to depict reality—correctly or incorrectly—are closely connected or even amount to the same thing. But this is not at all to say that for an elementary sentence to have sense is for it to be matched by an individual and corresponding *Sachverhalt*.

We are left, then, with the general proposal that, according to Wittgenstein, for an elementary sentence to have sense there must be a corresponding *Sachverhalt*. In the 4.2's where the expression 'elementary sentence' is introduced, Wittgenstein says:

> The simplest kind of sentence, an elementary sentence, is the existence of a *Sachverhalt*. [T 4.21]

> If an elementary sentence is true, the *Sachverhalt* exists: if an elementary sentence is false, the *Sachverhalt* does not exist. [T 4.25]

The latter remark, which amounts to (2), is corroborated by Wittgenstein's letter to Russell quoted above in which he says 'Sachverhalt is what corresponds to an Elementarsatz if it is true': when an elementary sentence is true there exists a corresponding *Sachverhalt*, and when it is false there does not exist such a *Sachverhalt*. Thus we have it from these sources that the existence or otherwise of a *Sachverhalt* corresponding to a picture *varies with* the truth-value of the picture, while we have it from T 2.22 and 2.221, quoted above, that the sense of a picture is *independent* of its truth-value. An elementary sentence with sense may well be false, and if so there will not exist a corresponding *Sachverhalt*, contrary to (1): the existence of a corresponding *Sachverhalt* is not a necessary condition of an elementary sentence's having sense. Thus if we are to give a consistent interpretation to the *Tractatus*, we cannot attribute (1) to Wittgenstein: we cannot attribute to him the doctrine that for an elementary sentence to have sense there must exist a corresponding *Sachverhalt*.

In conclusion: according to the argument considered above, (1) is a Tractarian doctrine, and therefore (2) should not be attributed to Wittgenstein. On examination we find that (2) is a Tractarian doctrine, and that (1) is not only inconsistent with (2), but is unsupported by the text.

Summary

The view that *Sachverhalte* are intended to be possibilities is not supported by Stenius' argument, nor by the argument above based on the assumption that in order for an elementary sentence to have sense there must exist a corresponding *Sachverhalt*. This is not to say that it is always perfectly clear what Wittgenstein meant in the relevant sections of the *Tractatus*, but the stronger and clearer evidence attaches to the view that *Sachverhalte* are intended as the actual, ontologically simple facts of which *Tatsache* are composed.

Accordingly, *Sachverhalt* has been translated above as 'elementary fact', though wherever this appears, 'configuration of objects' can be substituted. *Tatsache* is translated simply as 'fact', this being understood as a compound of elementary facts. The terms 'atomic' and 'molecular' are reserved for logical usage, to indicate the absence or presence of logical constants or objects.

Satz and *Elementarsatz*

The German term *Satz* carries as its main connotation the idea of a written or spoken declarative sentence, and a subsidiary connotation of the word is that of the meaning or thought expressed by a written or spoken sentence.

In Pears and McGuinness' and Ogden's translations of the *Tractatus Satz* and *Elementarsatz* are rendered as 'proposition' and 'elementary proposition'. Now 'proposition' in English is ambiguous in a similar way to *Satz* in German (though the relative weights of the two relevant connotations are somewhat different). It might seem therefore, that 'proposition' is the best translation. However, it is clear that Wittgenstein intended—at least most of the time—in his use of *Satz* to indicate a sentence, or sentence-type, as opposed to a meaning of some sort which comes between sentence and fact (see Black, *Companion*, p98ff). He speaks for example of words appearing in a *Satz* (T 2.0122), and of a *Satz* as 'set out on a printed page' (T 4.011). And regarding *Elementarsätze*, Wittgenstein says:

> An elementary sentence consists of names. It is a nexus, a concatenation, of names. [T 4.22; cf 5.55]

Here again we are dealing with names, which are syntactic entities, and not with meanings; and since *Sätze* reduce to *Elementarsätze*, this gives us further reason to think that Tractarian *Sätze* are syntactic entities—that they are sentences rather than meanings of sentences.

Regarding the option of translating *Elementarsatz* as 'atomic sentence', the point made above about elementary facts applies here also. An *Elementarsatz* is what is capable of depicting a *Sachverhalt*, and so it will share the character of a *Sachverhalt*. Wittgenstein argues that *Sachverhalte* are logically simple, and so it follows that *Elementarsätze* will also be logically simple. (And from this it also follows that *Elementarsätze* cannot contradict one another—see chapter 5.) But this is not a matter of the definition of *Elementarsatz* or *Sachverhalt*, and so should not be implied by the English translations of these terms: since the word 'atomic' carries the connotation of logical simplicity, it is inappropriate.

Thus, chosing 'elementary' rather then 'atomic', and 'sentence' rather than 'proposition', *Satz* and *Elementarsatz* have been translated here as 'sentence' and 'elementary sentence'.

Bibliography

Works by Wittgenstein

'Notes on Logic', 1913. In *Notebooks 1914-1918*, as Appendix I.

Notebooks 1914-1918, G.H. von Wright and G.E.M. Anscombe eds, 2nd ed., Oxford, Blackwell, 1979.

Prototractatus, B.F. McGuinness, T. Nyberg, and G.H. von Wright eds, London, RKP, 1971.

'Logisch-philosophische Abhandlung', in *Annalen den Naturphilosophie*, Wilhelm Ostwald ed., *Band* 14, *Heft* 3-4, pp184-262, Leipzig, Verlag Unesma GmbH, 1921.

Tractatus Logico-Philosophicus, C.K. Ogden trans., London, RKP, 1922. [Translation of *Logisch-philosophische Abhandlung.*]

Tractatus Logico-Philosophicus, D.F. Pears and B.F. McGuinness trans., London, RKP, 1961. [Translation of *Logisch-philosophische Abhandlung.*]

'Lecture on Ethics', in *Philosophical Review*, vol. 74, 1965.

'Remarks on Logical Form', in *Knowledge, Experience, and Realism*, Aristotelian Society Supplementary Volume, London, Harrison, 1929.

Philosophical Investigations, G.E.M. Anscombe trans., 2nd ed., Oxford, Blackwell, 1958.

Philosophical Remarks, Rush Rhees ed., Oxford, Blackwell, 1975.

Philosophical Grammar, Rush Rhees ed., A. Kenny trans., Oxford, Blackwell, 1974.

Culture and Value, G.H. von Wright ed., P. Winch trans., Oxford, Blackwell, 1980.

Zettel, G.E.M. Anscombe and G.H. von Wright eds, G.E.M. Anscombe trans., Oxford, Blackwell, 1967.

Wittgenstein's Letters

Letters to C.K. Ogden, G.H. von Wright ed., Oxford, Blackwell, 1973.

Letters to Russell, Keynes, and Moore, G.H. von Wright ed., Oxford, Blackwell, 1974.

Letters from Ludwig Wittgenstein, with a Memoir, Paul Englemann, Oxford, Blackwell, 1967.

Notes

'Notes Dictated to G.E. Moore in Norway', in *Notebooks 1914–1916*, pp 108–119, as Appendix II. [Dictated 1914.]

Ludwig Wittgenstein and the Vienna Circle: Conversations Recorded by Friedrich Waismann, B.F. McGuinness ed., Oxford, Blackwell, 1979. [Recorded 1929–32.]

'Wittgenstein's Lectures 1930–33', in G.E. Moore, *Philosophical Papers*, London, George Allen and Unwin Ltd., 1959.

Wittgenstein's Lectures, Cambridge 1930–1932, Desmond Lee ed., Oxford, Blackwell, 1980.

Wittgenstein's Lectures, Cambridge 1932–1935, Alice Ambrose ed., Oxford, Blackwell, 1982.

Other Works

Anscombe G.E.M. *An Introduction to Wittgenstein's* Tractatus, 2nd ed., London, Hutchinson, 1963.

Ashton D. *Twentieth Century Artists on Art*, New York, Pantheon Books, 1985.

Baker G. P. and Hacker P.M.S. *Wittgenstein: Meaning and Understanding*, Oxford, Blackwell, 1980.

Bell C. *Art*, London, 1914.

Black M. *A Companion to Wittgenstein's* 'Tractatus', Cambridge, CUP, 1964.

Blake, W. *Poetry and Prose of William Blake*, Nonesuch Press, London, 1939.

Bradley F.H. *Appearance and Reality*, 2nd ed., 1897.

Chadwick J.A. 'Logical Constants', *Mind*, vol. 36, pp1–11, 1927.

Clark, A. *Microcognition: Philosophy, Cognitive Science, and Parallel Distributed Processing*, London, MIT Press, 1989.

Dennett D.C. *Brainstorms: Philosophical Essays on Mind and Psychology*, Brighton, Harvester, 1981.

Dreyfus H. and Dreyfus S. *Mind over Machine*, Oxford, Blackwell, 1986.

Fodor J.A. *The Language of Thought*, New York, Crowell, 1975.

Fogelin R.J. *Wittgenstein*, London, RKP, 1976.

Fogelin R.J. 'Wittgenstein's Operator *N*', in *Analysis*, pp124–7,1982.

Frege G. 'What is a Function', in *Translations from the Writings of Gottlob Frege*, P. Geach and M. Black eds, Oxford, Blackwell, 1977.

Frege G. *Conceptual Notation and Related Articles*, T. Bynum ed., 1972.

Fry R. *Vision and Design*, London, 1920.

Gardner H. *The Mind's New Science: A History of the Cognitive Revolution*, New York, Basic Books, 1985.

Geach P.T. *Mental Acts*, London, Routledge, 1957.

Geach P.T. 'Wittgenstein's Operator *N*', in *Analysis*, pp168–170,1981.

Geach P.T. 'More on Wittgenstein's Operator *N*', in *Analysis*, pp127–8, 1982.

Goldwater R. and Treves M. eds. *Artists on Art*, London, John Murray, 1976.

Grattan-Guinness I. *Dear Russell – Dear Jourdain*, London, Duckworth, 1977.

Griffin J. *Wittgenstein's Logical Atomism*, Oxford, Blackwell, 1964.

Hacker P.M.S. *Insight and Illusion*, Oxford, Clarendon Press, 1972.

Heil J. 'Does Cognitive Psychology Rest on a Mistake?', in *Mind*, vol. XC, pp321–342, 1981.

Hertz H. *Electric Waves*, D.E. Jones trans., New York, Dover, 1962. [Original 1893]

Hertz H. *The Principles of Mechanics*, D.E. Jones and J.T. Walley trans., New York, Dover, 1956. [Original 1899]

Hintikka M.B. and Hintikka J. *Investigating Wittgenstein*, Oxford, Blackwell, 1985.

Hofmannsthal, H von. 'Ein Brief' in *Sämtliche Werke*, Frankfurt am Main, Fischer, 1984.

Hofmannsthal, H von. 'The Letter of Lord Chandos' in *Selected Prose*, M. Hottinger, T. Stern, J. Stern trans., pp 129–141, London, RKP, 1952. [translation of Hofmannsthal,1984]

Homer. *Odyssey*, New York, Harper and Row, 1965.

Humphreys C. *Zen Buddhism*, London, George Allen and Unwin, 1949.

James W. *The Varieties of Religious experience*, London, Longman Green & Co., 1952.

Janik A. and Toulmin S. *Wittgenstein's Vienna*, New York, Touchstone, 1973.

Johnson W.E. *Logic* (3 vols), Cambridge, 1921–4.

Kandinsky W. *Über das Geistige in der Kunst*, Munich, R. Piper Verlag, 1912.

Kandinsky W. *Concerning the Spiritual in Art*, Sadler M. trans., New York, Dover, 1977. [translation of Kandinsky, 1912]

Kandinsky W. and Marc F. ed.s. *Der Blaue Reiter*, Munich, R. Piper Verlag, 1912.

Kandinsky W. 'On the Question of Form', in *The* Blaue Reiter *Almanac*, Kandinsky W. and Marc F. ed.s, Falkenstein H. trans., London, Thames and Hudson, 1974. [Translation of Kandinsky and Marc, 1912]

Kant I. *Critique of Pure Reason*, London, Macmillan, 1961.

Kapp E. *Greek Foundations of Traditional Logic*, New York, AMS, 1967.

Kenny A. *Wittgenstein*, London, Penguin, 1973.

Kenny A. 'Wittgenstein on the Nature of Philosophy', in *Wittgenstein and his Times*, B. McGuinness ed., Oxford, Blackwell, 1982.

Klee P. *Paul Klee on Modern Art*, P. Findlay trans., London, Faber and Faber, 1948.

Kowalski R. *Logic for Problem Solving*, New York, Elsevier, 1979.

Lao Tzu. *Tao Te Ching*, D.C. Lau trans., London, Penguin, 1963.

Malcolm N. *Ludwig Wittgenstein: A Memoir, with a Biographical Sketch by G.H. von Wright*, 2nd ed., Oxford, OUP, 1984.

McGuinness B. 'The *Grundgedanke* of the *Tractatus*', in *Understanding Wittgenstein*, G. Vesey ed., London, Macmillan, 1984.

McGuinness B. *Wittgenstein: A Life (Young Ludwig 1889–1921)*, London, Duckworth, 1988.

Mondrian P. 'Plastic Art and Pure Plastic Art', in *The New Art—The New Life: The Collected Writings of Piet Mondrian*, Holtzmann H. and James M.S. trans. and ed.s, London, Thames and Hudson, 1986.

Moore G.E. *Philosophical Studies*, London, RKP, 1922.

Mounce H.O. *Wittgenstein's* Tractatus, Oxford, Blackwell, 1981.

Newell A. and Simon H. A. 'Computer Science as an Empirical Enquiry', *Communications of the Association for Computing Machinery*, 19, pp113–126, 1976.

Pears D. *The False Prison*, vol. 1, Oxford, Clarendon Press, 1987.

Peterson D.M. 'Logical Space and Truth-Functionality', in *The Tasks of Contemporary Philosophy: Reports of the Tenth International Wittgenstein Symposium*, A. Leinfellner and M. Wuketits eds, Hölder-Pichler-Tempsky, Vienna, 1986.

Peterson D.M. 'Wittgenstein's *Grundgedanke* and the Independence Thesis', in *Philosophical Investigations*, 1986.

Post E.L. 'Introduction to the General Theory of Elementary Propositions', *American Journal of Mathematics*, vol. 43, pp163–185, 1921.

Potts T.C. 'The Place of Structure in Communication', in *Communication and Understanding*, G. Vesey ed., Sussex, Harvester, 1977.

Ramsey F.P. *Foundations : Essays in Philosophy, Logic, Mathematics, and Economics*, D.H. Mellor ed., London, RKP, 1978.

Read H. *The Philosophy of Modern Art*, London, Faber and Faber, 1964.

Russell B. 'On Denoting', *Mind*, 14, 1905.

Russell B. 'Theory of Knowledge', in *The Collected Works of Bertrand Russell*, vol. 7, London, George Allen and Unwin, 1984. [Original written in 1913]

Russell B. *Our Knowledge of the External World*, London, George Allen and Unwin, 1914.

Russell B. *Mysticism and Logic*, Longmans, London, 1918.

Russell B. 'Philosophy of Logical Atomism', *Monist*, no.s 28–29, 1918–19.

Russell B. *Introduction to Mathematical Philosophy*, London, George Allen and Unwin, 1919.

Russell B. *The Principles of Mathematics*, 2nd ed., London, George Allen and Unwin, 1937.

Ryle G. 'Systematically Misleading Expressions', *Proceedings of the Aristotelian Society*, vol. 32, pp139–70, 1931–32.

Sextus Empiricus. *Sextus Empiricus with an English Translation*, R. G. Bury trans., 4 vols, Cambridge, Mass., Harvard University Press, 1933–49.

Sheffer H.M. 'A Set of Independent Postulates for Boolean Algebras', in *Transactions of the American Mathematical Society*, vol. XIV, pp481–8, 1913.

Smolensky P. 'On the Proper Treatment of Connectionism', *Behavioural and Brain Sciences*, 11, pp1–74, 1988.

Soames S. 'Generality, Truth Functions, and Expressive Capacity in the Tractatus', *The Philosophical Review*, XCII, no. 4, October 1983.

Stenius E. *Wittgenstein's* Tractatus: *A Critical Exposition of its Main Lines of Thought*, Conneticut, Greenwood Press, 1981.

Valéry P. *The Collected Works of Paul Valéry*, vol. 12, New York, Pantheon Books, 1960.

Whitehead A.N. and Russell B. *Principia Mathematica to *56*, Cambridge, CUP, 1962. [Original 1910–13]

Worringer W. *Abstraktion und Einfühlung: Ein Beitrag zur Stilpsychologie*, Munich, R. Piper Verlag, 1908.

Worringer W. *Abstraction and Empathy*, M. Bullock trans., New York, International Universities Press, 1953. [translation of Worringer, 1908]

Index